Connect to Love

Also by M. Gary Neuman

*The Truth about Cheating: Why Men Stray and
What You Can Do to Prevent It*

*In Good Times and Bad: Strengthening Your
Relationship When the Going Gets Tough*

*How to Make a Miracle: Finding Incredible
Spirituality in Times of Struggle and Happiness*

*Emotional Infidelity: How to Affair-Proof Your
Marriage and 10 Other Secrets to a Great
Relationship*

*Helping Your Kids Cope with Divorce the
Sandcastles Way*

Connect to Love

The Keys to Transforming
Your Relationship

M. Gary Neuman

WILEY

John Wiley & Sons, Inc.

Published by John Wiley & Sons, Inc., Hoboken, New Jersey
Published simultaneously in Canada

Design and composition by Forty-five Degree Design LLC

For general information about our other products and services, please contact our Customer Care Department within the United States at (800) 762-2974, outside the United States at (317) 572-3993 or fax (317) 572-4002.

Wiley also publishes its books in a variety of electronic formats. Some content that appears in print may not be available in electronic books. For more information about Wiley products, visit our web site at www.wiley.com.

Library of Congress Cataloging-in-Publication Data:

Neuman, M. Gary.
   Connect to love : the keys to transforming your relationship / M. Gary Neuman.
      p. cm.
   Includes index.
   ISBN 978-0-470-49156-0 (hardback); ISBN 978-0-470-65100-1 (ebk);
ISBN 978-0-470-65127-8 (ebk); ISBN 978-0-470-65128-5 (ebk)
 1. Man-woman relationships. I. Title.
   HQ801.N468 2010
   646.7'8—dc22

Printed in the United States of America

10 9 8 7 6 5 4 3 2 1

For the four great women in my life, with much
love and gratitude:

My mother, Celia

My mother-in-law, Rochelle

My wife, Melisa

My daughter, Esther

CONTENTS

Part Three: Connecting to Love for Good

PREFACE

There I was, sitting with Oprah on her set discussing my book *The Truth about Cheating: Why Men Stray and What You Can Do to Prevent It*. For over twenty-three years, I've worked to help couples through significant problems in their relationships. My goal has always been to develop healthier attitudes and genuine loving connections between partners. When I wrote *The Truth about Cheating*, I was excited about exploring the inner thoughts of faithful and unfaithful men in a study of two hundred men throughout the United States. I knew it would be empowering for women to know what their men were thinking, yet not sharing, on the topic of faithfulness. Some women asked me, "What about us and our cheating and unhappiness?"

I felt that having the key to what makes men tick in relationships would only improve women's chances for happiness in their relationships. I announced on the show that I was in the process of doing comprehensive research on the faithfulness of women—or lack thereof. It was a long-avoided topic, and I wanted to explore what women were thinking and feeling in their relationships and how they could get their needs and desires met. This book reveals the results of that research. Over five hundred women from around the world have spoken, giving me the opportunity to share their deepest feelings and struggles.

Research has significantly changed with the Internet, which offers an unmatched anonymity that translates to more honest answers today than researchers might have been able to get in the past. Especially when dealing with such a subject as marital dissatisfaction and female cheating, anonymity is essential. I created my research questions with the assistance of a college professor and others at the university and posted them online. I considered where I could best hear a collective female voice. I was fortunate to be granted permission to use Oprah.com, which graciously created a link to my study so that women visiting that site could participate in it. In a separate study, I conducted face-to-face interviews with women from a parenting class in South Florida, where I live. Finally, several additional Web sites linked to my research questions after the link on Oprah.com closed. I then had three different sources of information that I could compare to see if I was receiving similar information from each. I found the results to be the same in all three groups, which gave me confidence that the research represented the genuine views of a cross-section of women.

I wanted to find clear, practical solutions for men and women to make their relationships much better. I needed to find the actions you could take that would work and, just as important, which ones would not work. I wanted to discover the few most influential ways to make an incredible difference in your marriage.

To accomplish this, I developed two survey questionnaires: one for women involved in extramarital affairs and one for those who were faithful. The only prerequisite for women taking one of the two surveys was that they had to be or have been married; the reason for this was to avoid any confusion about the definition of "cheating." I also found out how many women felt their infidelity led to divorce. The faithful survey had fifty-two questions and the unfaithful survey had sixty-seven. If you take these numbers and add the fact that most of the questions had multiple responses (where women were asked to supply percentage values for all options that applied), then multiply by the 505 individual women who took the survey, you will see that you are the beneficiary of more than 100,000 total responses. The participants represent every state in the United States—plus there's a voice from other parts of the world, including Europe, South America, Canada, Australia, and Africa. Different ages, races, and incomes are all represented.

This research has been presented at an international psychological conference and is being submitted for publication in psychological journals. The stories are eye-opening. The results are surprising. The answers this collective female voice offers all of us—both women and men—are practical and meaningful.

ACKNOWLEDGMENTS

To Oprah Winfrey, thank you for allowing me to use Oprah.com to assist with this research and for helping me help others.

To Professor Matthew Sachs, PhD, for your crucial assistance in this study. Thank you for representing my work at psychological conventions and for your tireless efforts to help me develop the research and create a reliable and valid measure. You have been wonderful to work with. We made a great team, and I hope we can team up again for future projects.

To my daughter, Esther, thanks for your incredible help with this research. Your management of the study and of the women who participated was wise and warm. I couldn't have done it without you.

To Carol Mann, thank you for making it all happen and for your calmness and efficiency.

To Tom Miller, thanks for the endless time you've put into this book and for caring so much about its message. Your efforts are much appreciated.

To Rachel Meyers, thanks for your thoughtful and great copy-editing of this book.

To Ronni Stolzenberg and Betsy Hulsebosh at Launchpad 360, thanks for all of your help in bringing my message to others.

To Kitt Allan, Laura Cusack, and Mike Onorato, thank you for your constant effort and genuine care of this book.

To Robin Landers, thanks for your humor and insights, for reading and editing the manuscript, and for provoking many discussions about men and women since the dawn of womankind. You are always thrilled to help out, and it is so appreciated.

To my friends and family who gave of their time and insights:

Sherri and Jeff, Barbara and Craig, Jill and David, Karen and Peter, Nancy and Marty, for being there at all times.

Robin Jacobs, for working with me to advance my message and for your unique take on life.

Dr. Alfred Jonas, I continue to strive to live up to your example of humility, kindness, and psychological insight.

Rick Hirsch, for the journalist's insight into how the world works.

Allan Rosenthal, Esq., thank you for always returning my calls and answering questions with the wisdom of your life experience. You are a true friend to my family.

Sandy Rosenblum, Esq., for all of your help and generosity of time and spirit.

The Weill family and all of my friends at G.V. Thank you for listening to my findings, always providing great feedback, and endless hospitality.

Bonnie, for always being there.

Many thanks to my children, Yehuda, Esther, Michael, Pacey, and Danny for being so kind and interested in the myriad discussions surrounding the writing of this book. Your mother and I love you and are proud of each of you. We are so blessed to have you for our children, and now you've grown into my best friends.

To the One above, who makes all things possible.

Introduction

This is a book for couples about what women want in their relationships. It is not a book about women and cheating. I hope to help couples prevent infidelity, but my main goal is to share what I've learned from the courageous women, happy and sad, who've revealed their highly personal thoughts and feelings. Through listening to the collective voice of these women, every couple can discover meaningful, practical changes that are sure to make their love relationships far more loving, romantic, and intimate. Women and men will gain a deeper insight into what a woman needs from love and what both partners can do to make their relationship great.

You are about to hear the voices of over five hundred women. Through exhaustive research, I have worked to bring you a clearer, deeper understanding about women and love. Both men and women have a great deal to learn about love. By writing this book, I wanted to help everyone understand what women want from their relationships.

As you'll soon learn, the vast majority of women are profoundly unhappy in their relationships. Sadly, 39 percent of the women in my study have reported physically cheating, and the majority of them have never admitted it to their mates. Equally surprising is that over half of the faithful women in my research said they had seriously considered separation or divorce within the past year. Only 30 percent of women were both faithful and happy in their relationships.

The common thinking is that men cheat far more than women. Clearly, everyone may be willing to consider that female cheating is on the rise, but most still think it doesn't happen that often. I suppose we believe that compared to men, women are more dedicated partners, have less of a sex drive, or surely don't want sex for the sake of sex. Some assume that women are simply conditioned to follow the role of wife and mother, even if that role isn't bringing them much happiness.

My last book refuted many myths about men and their cheating patterns. Of the two hundred men I studied, a hundred had cheated on their wives and a hundred had remained faithful. When I asked the unfaithful men about the reasons they were dissatisfied in their marriages at the time of their affairs, I expected sexual dissatisfaction to either top the list or be near the top. When only 8 percent reported that factor to have been the problem, compared to 48 percent who declared emotional dissatisfaction to have been the primary issue, I was dumbfounded. What about the idea that men are pigs who seek as much sex as possible? Clearly, men have far more emotional needs than most assume. But the idea that many men cheat seems to be a given.

When I began this study about women, everyone around me had definite opinions as well. The thought seemed almost unanimous that when women cheat, it's not for the sex. And many believed that women don't really cheat much at all. But a few told me that women cheat much more than everyone thinks, and they were almost indignant that people think of cheating as primarily a male activity. Statements such as "We need sex too" seemed to proclaim a desire for equality by many women who were tired of books that focus on what women should be thinking about in a marriage while men are given a free ride.

I was concerned that I wouldn't be able to find enough female cheaters to have a good sample. I wanted at least one hundred cheaters. But it soon became apparent that this wouldn't be a problem. The 39 percent rate of cheating was so high and so far beyond my expectations, I became concerned that people wouldn't believe it. I redid my study twice in smaller form with different populations, and only felt completely comfortable when all three studies yielded similar results. Ultimately, my three studies combined included 505 women.

One recent University of Washington study reported that 28 percent of men cheat and only 15 percent of women cheat and claimed that female cheating was up from 5 percent twenty years ago. There have been other studies that showed male cheating to be much higher than 28 percent, so there seems to be a lot of wiggle room with these numbers.

Why do people mistakenly think women rarely cheat? Perhaps the answer is, as the Rutgers anthropologist Helen Fisher has explained, "Men want to think women don't cheat, and women want men to think they don't cheat. Therefore, the sexes have been playing a little psychological game with each other." As

David C. Atkins, PhD, a University of Washington research asso-
ciate professor, said when evaluating his own university statistics,
"Women underreport affairs in face-to-face studies, so real numbers are likely three times higher." My own research shows that
he's right.

A further part of my research ultimately gave me my answer.
Thirty-eight percent of the cheaters said that their husbands had
never questioned them about their cheating and they had never
told their husbands about their infidelity. Twenty-four percent
stated that they had lied to their husbands even after their
husbands had discovered some evidence of a relationship but not
hard evidence of actual sex. In other words, 62 percent of husbands who have cheating wives either have never even discussed
it or have been flatly told that their suspicions are wrong.
That's why everyone thinks women cheat much less than they do.
Whatever percentage you thought was accurate for cheating
women, just add in all of those women whose men haven't a clue
or at least have never brought it up. Suddenly 39 percent becomes
credible.

When an unfortunate double standard became apparent during the study, I discovered another reason for the secrecy surrounding female infidelity. I began putting together a list of
women who had been unfaithful and would be willing to discuss
their experiences in the media. It became increasingly difficult
to find them. Each one had an understandable reason for not
sharing their story in public, such as "My husband would be
mortified and shamed" or "I work as a teacher/in radio/as an exec-
utive and it would threaten my job." In the past, when I had
looked for unfaithful men to discuss their infidelity, there wasn't
any shortage of men willing to be open about their experiences.
In fact, many men admitted that their business associates were
familiar with their indiscretions. Evidently, the world is a signifi-

cantly harsher judge of female infidelity. Sadly, this societal gag order has led women to silence their public voice, forgoing their right to express their deep need for genuine loving connections in their marriages and how painful it is when their needs aren't being met.

The fact that more than half of faithful women are so unhappy in their relationships tells us there is significant work that needs to be done to improve our love relationships. Regardless of how you view the research, the message is clear: many women are unhappy and feel lonely in their relationships. How can we address these issues in the most effective way? That is the question I intend to answer in the pages that follow.

I'll also reveal some crucial facts about women who are happy in their relationships—like how they spend twice as much time talking daily with their mates and have twice as much sex than women who are faithful but profoundly dissatisfied in their relationships.

When I asked happily married women why they think they haven't cheated, the number one answer (75 percent) was that they work hard on their marriage and feel close to their husbands. Clearly, chances for a happy relationship seriously increase when both spouses are tending to it.

When they start out in a serious love relationship, most women never dream of getting to a place where they want to exit the relationship or cheat on the man they once loved. Yet most women have been there. This book is committed to helping women never get to that point again.

Women's Voices

We all enjoy hearing from others like ourselves about their experiences. It helps us to develop deeper insights into why we feel the way we do, and to learn from one another how we can communicate the changes we want to see in our love relationships. This book seeks to meet that need by offering women 505 female voices to listen to that provide details never touched on before.

Many of the women in my study reported that they were so lost in their relationships that they couldn't begin to properly break down the problems in order to start fixing them. They had difficulty identifying, evaluating, and articulating the specific issues that were bothering them. Others admitted to hiding from much of the sadness they felt, since they had no way of knowing how to deal with it. These women appreciated participating in the research because it helped them identify the specific details of what they were feeling, which they needed to fully understand in order to make things better.

The Truth about Female Cheating and Unhappiness

Faithful and unfaithful women who believed they'd never cheat: 85%

Faithful women who have seriously considered separation or divorce in the last year: 51%

Women who have cheated: 39%

Cheating women who have never been asked about it or have lied even after there was some evidence: 62%

Both women who were faithful but unhappy and women who were unfaithful said they wished they could better communicate their needs to their husbands. They lamented that they were not clear enough inside themselves about exactly what was making them so sad. And they felt unable to get their points across to their husbands so that their husbands would understand and join them in making changes. Rather than talking with their husbands using a healthy "here are the serious issues" approach, they admitted to shouting complaints at their husbands or acting them out emotionally. They didn't have the clarity to outline their issues and to calmly discuss how they and their husbands might change their behavior toward each other.

There could be many reasons for having difficulty communicating. But I know it always helps convince a man when he hears many other people saying the same thing his wife is saying. Many women complain that their opinions are not taken as seriously by their husbands until someone else gives the same opinion. I'm not suggesting this is the right attitude. It's not, and by discussing it here I hope to help husbands change. But for now, introducing them to the hundreds of women internationally who are speaking in one voice will have a greater impact and give them more inspiration to listen up and consider how to make their wives happier.

Men Hearing Women

If you are a man, congratulations on picking up this book (even if your wife read it through first and gave it to you). It is a well-known fact that most men do not read self-help relationship books. Unfortunately, this causes a vicious cycle: fewer books are written for men, which leads to less help offered to men, ultimately supporting the claim that men are less skilled than women at creating healthy relationships.

Indeed, men are commonly thought to lag far behind women in the Knowing How to Make a Relationship Great department. We tend to focus on many things other than our wives. Business and money might top the list for many, followed by kids and sports mixed in there somewhere. The simple question you want to ask yourself is, "Where does my partner fit into my personal life picture?"

If a woman is asked to describe herself, likely the first or second thing she'll say whether if she is a wife or a mother. If you ask a man the same question, he's likely to start off describing his job title or saying he's a dad. It's unlikely he will mention he's a husband first or second. That fact may not even make the short list. Likewise, it's not uncommon for women to wonder who they'll marry one day, and how many children they'll have, while men tend to wonder what job they'll have, how much money they'll make, and how they will enjoy themselves.

It's no wonder the cliché developed that women are the driving force behind a marriage, while men don't get the whole relationship thing. It's not because men don't care about their wives. Not at all. If there is one thing I learned from my study of men, it is that they desperately want to feel like winners at home and please their wives. They are willing to make changes and diligently work toward making their relationships better and their wives happier. But that doesn't mean they're actively searching for the ways to make that happen. Whether because of their genes or their social conditioning, they are not easily attuned to considering how to improve their relationships. Men seem far more attuned to jokes about the amount of sex they're not getting with their wives, how business is going, and talk about cars and sports teams.

I hope this book will speak to that inner part of every man that does want to be a winner at home and have a loving, passionate relationship. Men will find that this book offers researched, concise answers about how to improve their love relationships.

Some had suggested to me that I consider writing a book aimed solely at women. I thought, a study about women and what they need, written just for women? Huh. Curious. I couldn't help but agree with what I perceived as the question of every woman walking the face of the earth: "Aren't men ever going to be held accountable for their part in relationships?"

There's a joke about a husband who believes his wife is cheating on him. He hires a private investigator, and within a day the PI calls to set up a meeting; he already has information. He shows his client photos of his wife with another man. There they are cheering in the stands at a baseball game. A second photo shows the two of them playing pool later the same day in a sports bar. A third photo shows them dancing on the table of a club late that same night.

"I can't believe it," the husband spits out.

"Many men are shocked that their wives are cheating."

To which the husband responds, "No, I'm not surprised she's cheating. . . . I just didn't know she could have so much fun."

This joke is poignant, because while none of us finds cheating excusable, we recognize that we behave differently with different people. It takes two to make a relationship great or lousy. Each of us should consider our role in creating a wonderful or a disconnected relationship. We hope this husband wonders what the other man is doing that makes his wife so happy.

It is every man's role to do his part in creating a successful relationship. Love relationships, like business and sports, may not always be successful, but without good energy and focus there is no chance of success. I appeal to every man who is in a relationship to consider my message. Men have incredible capabilities in the area of love and emotions, and now is a time of great change. In one generation, men have become more nurturing fathers than ever before. Men have shown that they can step away from stereotypes and care deeply about their loved ones, regardless of how they were brought up. You must now make a decision to take the steps to become a man who is truly invested in making his relationship great. As you read through this book, I hope you will follow its practical suggestions and see solid, positive changes in your relationship. Be open to the possibilities that exist for you and the woman you love.

This Book Will Help You Change Your Relationship

Change is the most beautiful part of our being human. It is not simply that our ability to adapt makes us wonderful, but that our willingness to look within to improve who we are truly makes us unique individuals. There is a taste of spirituality in the will and determination to better who we are and to love those around us. It is the shining trait of the human spirit.

Ideally, couples will gain from reading this book simultaneously, but one partner alone can also learn and dramatically make his or her relationship better by following its practical ideas. I'm a big believer in people taking control of themselves and using their sole actions to change the energy in their relationships. Each of us can affect any relationship for better or for worse, so we don't have to wait for our spouse to see the light to begin making significant changes. I've addressed certain distinct male and female issues in two separate chapters for men and women, as well as in various sections throughout the book, in order to empower you to begin to make real changes to benefit your couplehood. Whether you are reading this as a couple or as an individual, you can make the difference.

Though the discussion refers primarily to husbands and wives and the marital relationship, the information in this book is relevant to men and women in all committed relationships. When you conduct research, maintaining clarity is crucial to the validity of the study. For example, if women who had never been married said they once cheated, you'd rightfully question whether their version of cheating would match with your personal perspective. Were the women in "committed" relationships and what would define a "commitment"? To avoid this confusion, my study focused on the experiences of married women so that we'd all agree on the definition of fidelity. However, what we learned from married women naturally applies to all couples in serious relationships. The deep feelings and desires and relationship dynamics discussed here apply to everyone. I chose to commonly use "husband," "wife," or "spouse" throughout this book in order to avoid the confusion by constantly switching between terms like lover, boyfriend, and girlfriend. This book is ultimately for all of us who genuinely search for meaningful love in our couplehood.

Throughout the book are personal stories that women shared with me during the interviews I conducted as part of my research. Identifying facts have been altered to protect their privacy, but the feelings and issues described are very much accurate. You will also read about many women who informally shared their own stories about their marriages, some who knew their husbands had cheated on them, as well. Beyond these real stories, there are some that have been created as composites. I do not share stories of clients who see me therapeutically, so any similarity between the stories in this book and people I have counseled is purely coincidental.

Let's Say It Right Now: I'm Not Assessing Blame

Perhaps you saw the frustration expressed by some women on *The Oprah Winfrey Show* about my earlier book *The Truth about Cheating.* Some women felt they were being blamed for the fact that men cheat, although others felt empowered by having the information offered in the book. As in that book, my intention here is only to open a genuine discussion about what individuals feel and how they experience their love relationships. The discussion must be open before I can suggest practical steps to help couples create wonderful relationships.

The Two-Week Connect to Love Program

I've spent over twenty-three years helping couples turn their relationships around. One of the programs I've developed is a Reconnect to Love Day, in which I work with a couple intensely for hours over a day or two, seeing them both together and individually. It's hard to imagine that dramatic change can occur in such a short time, but it does. Through my work as a clinician, I've heard a clear, collective voice expressing what couples want and where they can focus their energy to get the most positive results. I've taken some parts of this process and developed them into a two-week program couples can do on their own to help them make dramatic, positive changes in their relationships. Love is like atomic energy, unbelievably powerful. The trick is learning how to release that energy. Anyone can do that in a very short period of time.

No one can do it all, but now you no longer have to. Follow the few steps in this book, and your relationship and life will positively change dramatically and quickly.

PART ONE

Connecting to What Women Want

1

The Connect to Love
Questionnaire

No simple quiz can accurately take into account the unique circumstances of every relationship. This set of questions was developed based on the results reported in my study of women. It is meant to be the beginning of a conversation you may have with yourself and your partner. This quiz is not a true diagnostic tool as much as a general baseline by which to measure your situation.

Answer the questions in the section that applies to you, give the corresponding section to your partner, and then compare your answers. The answer key for both quizzes is on page 22.

Questions for Wives or Girlfriends

As I explained in the introduction, the information in this book applies to all partners in committed relationships. To avoid the confusion of alternating nouns, I have used "husband" through-out this quiz. If you are a girlfriend, please substitute "boyfriend" for "husband."

1. On average, each day, I spend this amount of time talking alone with my husband:
   a. _____ Five minutes or less
   b. _____ Five to fifteen minutes
   c. _____ Fifteen to thirty minutes
   d. _____ Thirty to sixty minutes
   e. _____ Over sixty minutes

2. On average, per month, I have sex with my husband:
   a. _____ Ten times or more
   b. _____ Six to ten times
   c. _____ Five times or fewer

3. I feel that my husband:
   a. _____ Appreciates me.
   b. _____ Somewhat appreciates me.
   c. _____ Does not appreciate me nearly enough.
   d. _____ Does not appreciate me.

4. I feel that:
   a. _____ My husband regularly understands me and talks to me about my feelings and thoughts.
   b. _____ My husband somewhat understands me and talks to me about my feelings and thoughts.

    c. _____ My husband often does not understand me or talk to me about my feelings and thoughts.

    d. _____ My husband regularly does not understand me or talk to me about my feelings and thoughts.

5. I feel that:

    a. _____ We do not spend enough time alone together.

    b. _____ We do spend enough time alone together.

    c. _____ We often spend alone time together but not nearly enough of it.

6. I feel that generally: (Choose one from each pair.)

    a. _____ Other aspects of my husband's life are more important to him than our relationship.

    b. _____ Other aspects of my husband's life are not more important to him than our relationship.

    a. _____ We are no longer interested in the same things.

    b. _____ We are still interested in the same things.

    a. _____ Sex is too infrequent.

    b. _____ Sex is frequent enough.

    a. _____ Sex is unsatisfying.

    b. _____ Sex is satisfying.

    a. _____ My husband demands too much sex.

    b. _____ My husband does not demand too much sex.

    a. _____ My husband has significantly neglected his appearance.

    b. _____ My husband has not significantly neglected his appearance.

7. My husband loses his temper and is moody and angry:
   a. ____ Often
   b. ____ Not often

8. In the past six months I have been angry at my husband:
   a. ____ A lot
   b. ____ Sometimes
   c. ____ Hardly
   d. ____ Not at all

Questions for Husbands or Boyfriends

As I explained in the introduction, the information in this book applies to all partners in committed relationships. To avoid the confusion of alternating nouns, I have used "wife" throughout this quiz. If you are a boyfriend, please substitute "girlfriend" for "wife."

1. On average, each day, I spend this amount of time talking alone with my wife:
   a. ____ Five minutes or less
   b. ____ Five to fifteen minutes
   c. ____ Fifteen to thirty minutes
   d. ____ Thirty to sixty minutes
   e. ____ Over sixty minutes

2. On average, per month, I have sex with my wife:
   a. ____ Ten times or more
   b. ____ Six to ten times
   c. ____ Five times or fewer

3. I believe that my wife feels:
    a. ____ Appreciated by me.
    b. ____ Somewhat appreciated by me.
    c. ____ Somewhat unappreciated by me.
    d. ____ Unappreciated by me.

4. I believe my wife feels that:
    a. ____ I regularly understand her and talk to her about her feelings and thoughts.
    b. ____ I somewhat understand her and talk to her about her feelings and thoughts.
    c. ____ I often do not understand her and talk to her about her feelings and thoughts.
    d. ____ I regularly do not understand her and talk to her about her feelings and thoughts.

5. My wife would say that:
    a. ____ We do not spend enough time alone together.
    b. ____ We do spend enough time alone together.
    c. ____ We often spend alone time together but not nearly enough of it.

6. My wife feels that (choose one from each pair):
    a. ____ Other aspects of my life are more important to me than our relationship.
    b. ____ Other aspects of my life are not more important to me than our relationship.

    a. ____ We are no longer interested in the same things.
    b. ____ We are still interested in the same things.

    a. ____ Sex is too infrequent.
    b. ____ Sex is frequent enough.

    a. ____ Sex is unsatisfying.

    b. ____ Sex is satisfying.

    a. ____ I demand too much sex.

    b. ____ I do not demand too much sex.

    a. ____ I have significantly neglected my appearance.

    b. ____ I have not significantly neglected my appearance.

7. I lose my temper and am moody and angry:

    a. ____ Often

    b. ____ Not often

8. In the past six months my wife has been angry at me:

    a. ____ A lot

    b. ____ Sometimes

    c. ____ Hardly

    d. ____ Not at all

Answer Key

  1. a-0, b-5, c-7, d-10

  2. a-10, b-5, c-0

  3. a-10, b-7, c-3, d-0

  4. a-10, b-7, c-3, d-0

  5. a-0, b-5, c-2

  6. a-0, b-3; a-0, b-1; a-0, b-3; a-0, b-2; a-0, b-1; a-0, b-1

  7. a-0, b-1

  8. a-0, b-4, c-10, d-10

If your score was:

55–66 points: Keep doing what you're doing and apply the principles outlined in the book to make your relationship even better.

30–55 points: You both need to put in work to be happy and satisfied in the relationship. Consider the Two-Week Reconnection Program to make things better quickly.

0–30 points: Unfortunately, it's likely you're experiencing profound sadness and immediate, focused attention is crucial to creating a happier relationship.

If both of you did your own questionnaire, compare your answers and see if they are the same. Identifying the similarities and differences will spark discussion on how each of you thinks your relationship is going.

2

Veronica's Story:
It's Complicated

Veronica's story introduces themes that were common in many stories I heard during my research. She loved her husband very much and their marriage was strong, but after many years her relationship lost its way and she grew restless and desperate to get more out of her life. Women like Veronica remind us to do the hard work that is necessary to improve our relationships as the alternatives can be personally devastating. You may get discouraged at times, but Veronica's story is proof that the hard work will bring big rewards. Here's Veronica in her own words:

Jack and I got married fairly young, at twenty-two and twenty-three. We both came from very similar families, with similar upbringings. We got married exactly two years from the date of our first official date. He was the man of my dreams: handsome, muscular, compassionate, caring, loving, virile, extremely affectionate verbally and physically, and motivated to make a wonderful life with me. Jack always treated me like a queen and often told me that all he wanted was to see me smile. I was going to college and working part-time when we got married. He was working for IBM fixing computers. We lived in an extremely small apartment, but we didn't care, we just wanted to be together. We were like any other young married couple. We had our share of arguments, but nothing major.

After almost two years of marriage, I graduated from college and we moved to Houston, where we were lucky that his company had an opening. After I got my teaching credential, we were able to buy the home of our dreams and move into a wonderful home and neighborhood. We are Christians, and so attending church was an important part of our lives. We had many newly married friends who were all along somewhat the same path as us in life. We had busy social lives, and family time was important to both of us.

After a few years of marriage, we wanted to start a family. We struggled through what we thought would be the hardest trial of our marriage: infertility. Jack stood by me through the testing and procedures with 100 percent support. After about a year of infertility treatments, we were blessed with a daughter. The month before she was born, Jack decided to go back to school, and he started online courses to earn his teaching degree, like me. I supported this decision wholeheartedly. He was working extremely hard, working a job that required odd hours at times, then juggling schoolwork and the demands of an online schedule, while wanting to be an involved dad and a supportive and loving husband.

This rigorous schedule for him went on for a year and a half. After a full day at work, Jack would come home and try to spend quality time with me and our daughter, before he had to go upstairs and work on the computer all night to fulfill his course requirements. We would put our daughter to bed by seven o'clock, and that was when we had our "separate" time. Jack would be on the computer doing schoolwork until all hours of the night, while I passed the time watching TV alone. When I went to bed, I found myself longing for the feeling of "butterflies in my stomach" and wanting to feel and remember what it was like to have the thrill of the chase. I have been cursed and blessed with an overactive imagination, so before I would fall asleep, I would find myself once again falling into my old habits of creating situations in my head where I could experience these long-lost feelings.

This went on for quite some time, and I could feel Jack and me growing apart, due to my fantasies and his long hours away from the family with work and school. It was like his new passion included everything in his life but me. I did not realize at the time that it was happening, but it was. He had lost touch with me and was too far away emotionally to try at all to be in love with me again. Jack had become a different person. I felt like I was begging for his attention. He'd make me feel like I was too needy, that I was selfish or something because I wanted some of that passion back. Even worse, he had become angrier than I had ever known him to be. I became afraid to even bring up to him how I was feeling. I began to question myself and wonder if I had become unattractive in every way.

An opportunity at work came up for me to go to Europe. I was hesitant because I didn't want to leave Jack and my eighteen-month-old daughter; however, I had never really been outside of Texas before. I taught English literature, and so badly wanted to go see the world and experience what I was teaching. Jack has always been supportive, and so he made it work for me to go. I was gone for eighteen days, while he stayed home juggling an eighteen-month-old while working and going to school full-time. While it was hard leaving my husband and daughter behind, I felt it was something I needed to do. When I got to the airport, I literally left God, Jack, and all my responsibilities at the check-in line. When I got to Europe, I felt so free. Free of the responsibilities of a wife, a teacher, and, mostly, a new mother. I hadn't had any real time for myself in the eighteen months since our daughter was born. I guess I didn't realize how much I had missed my "alone" time until I got to Europe.

We had a tour guide for the entire eighteen days on this trip. His name was Henry. He was funny, smart, cute, witty, single, and British. I soon found myself fantasizing about him. One night we went to a bar to karaoke with some of the students. I ended up drinking too much and found myself flirting with Henry. When we got back to the hotel around 2:00 a.m., I went to my room and found a note on the door from my roommate. It said we had cockroaches in our room, so we had switched and were now sharing with two other girls. When I got to our new room, there was no place for me to sleep and all the other girls were fast asleep, so I took it as an excuse to go to Henry's room.

When he opened the door, I told him what had happened and he invited me in. We ended up talking while we lay in bed: he on one side of the bed, and me on the other. We started sharing our personal feelings; neither of us wanted to have sex with our partners (he had a girlfriend at the time) anymore because the spark was gone. That conversation led to a kiss, which moved on to everything but sexual intercourse. I had fantasized about this so many times in my head, but when it came down to it, I remember thinking, "This is awkward. He is much skinnier than my husband; I don't fit right when I lay my head on his chest . . ." but I went ahead and did it anyway. All in all, it was about forty-five minutes before it was over. I had made it clear that I didn't want to have sex. I felt awkward after it was over, and decided to go back to my room.

In the morning, I felt like I was in a dream, and it was even more awkward to see him the next day. We talked during the next few days and said we would set up a time to be together again. When we were in Paris, we had a chance to sit alone at a restaurant and have a drink. I felt the sparks and felt like we were on a date. We were sharing intimate details about our lives. I remember trying to justify my situation. I asked him if he had ever seen *The Bridges of Madison County.* I really felt like that woman, and I vividly recall the scene in the movie where her husband comes back and she is in the truck with her husband while it's raining outside. Clint Eastwood's character is in the truck in front of theirs. She's debating whether or not to open the door and jump into his truck and leave her old life behind, or to stay in the truck with her husband and weather the storm. It's just a brief moment in the movie, but I often see her hand on the truck handle and feel the same pull. I don't think Henry had any clue what I was talking about because he wasn't married and did not have the responsibilities of a child. At the end of our "date" I was excited about the possibility of another rendezvous.

I approached him two more times during the trip, and he closed the door on me. At the time I was upset, I felt rejected and devastated, but now, I thank him for denying me for whatever reason.

Finally the trip came to an end, and when it was over, I was greeted at the airport with my loving husband, who had a dozen red roses for me and who had dressed our daughter in an adorable dress and had put her hair in pigtails. I don't think it really hit me then . . . not until the jet lag disappeared.

When I got back, Jack was so happy to have me home, he showered me with affection and attention. I started to feel the reality of what I had done. I was grieving the loss of my freedom from responsibilities, I was grieving the thought that I would never see Henry again, and I was realizing the tremendous mistake I made. I finally told Jack about my fling with Henry. For two years, he was angry at me and our relationship was sour. At this point in our lives I felt so ignored by Jack. Nothing had changed. He wasn't into me and nothing I did could seem to make him so. I tried to explain how distant he made me feel and how alone I was, but he couldn't hear it.

Finally, we decided to go to a marriage retreat. That was the hardest weekend our marriage has been through. We had to ask some really difficult questions and face the reality of our answers. At the end of that weekend, Jack told me he wanted to put the affair behind us and move forward. I was so relieved to hear him say that. From that time on, we were able to go forward. Jack had fully forgiven me, and his love and forgiveness allowed me to forgive myself. He began to accept how much he had been distant from me, and even though it wasn't an excuse for what I did, he promised he would never pull away from me again. Things were not perfect, but they were much, much better. A few months later, we talked about having another child. He said he was ready to move forward with our family. To our surprise, we got pregnant on our second try, without any infertility procedures or drugs.

When I was in my last trimester, Jack told me that he never thought he'd be able to fully love me again after the affair. He said that is why he did not want to have another child at first. He felt that he would only be able to live with me and love me on the surface for our daughter's sake, without fully giving himself to me. Having another child would mean that he was vulnerable again and deeply committed to fully loving me. When I looked at him in surprise for sharing this with me, I asked him how he felt now that I was pregnant, and he smiled and said, "Well it's obvious isn't it . . . I love you!"

After the birth of our second daughter, I told Jack that I wanted to honor him by telling some of our closest friends what had happened. I had blamed him over the past two years for our marital problems that were extremely obvious to our friends. To cover up the real issue, I told them that he was grouchy due to school and life. They had obviously noticed a change in his behavior for those two years after the affair. Jack did not want me to tell our friends for fear that they would judge me and treat me disrespectfully. I told him I was willing to take the risk because they needed to know the truth and I needed to accept responsibility.

We ended up telling a few of our closest friends, and in time, I went on to tell my sister and my mother. I am so blessed to be surrounded by such loving and caring friends and family, who so generously gave me their forgiveness as well. I am humbled to tell you that we have survived infertility and an affair within our thirteen years of marriage.

When you stand at the altar when you first get married and promise "for better or worse," you don't know at that moment what your "worse" will be. One of the things we learned through this is that love is not just a feeling, but a choice and a commitment. Feelings come and go, but a commitment sticks it out.

Now we only choose to tell people about the affair if there is a purpose. We want to be able to help struggling couples and to use our story to show people that marriage can survive an affair. I guarantee you it won't be easy, but if you can stick out the storm, the rainbow will appear in time.

3

Enjoy Your Time
Together

M ost people I spoke to about my study believed that women
would report that they were very unhappy or cheating
for emotional reasons and sex was a distant, secondary issue.
Generally, women are seen as the less sexual gender. Yes, we know
women enjoy sex, but most people assume they don't miss it the
way men do. If a man goes days or weeks without sex, it's
assumed he's going to explode. If the same happens to a woman,
somehow it's assumed she'll keep busy and not actively miss it.
Marital jokes are frequently about how little sex the husband is
getting. And I think I read somewhere that given a choice between

finding great shoes or having great sex, most women choose the shoes. Five hundred and five women from around the world say these assumptions are all wrong.

Among the women in my study, faithful wives who were unhappy in their marriages gave equal weight to sexual and emotional dissatisfaction as their primary issues. Likewise, with cheaters, the number one response when asked what issues factored into their infidelity was "Both emotional dissatisfaction and an unsatisfying sexual relationship figured about the same in my decision." Forty-four percent responded this way, almost double the number of women who answered that emotional issues were the driving force (26 percent). Similar to my study of men, only 7 percent said that it was largely sexual dissatisfaction that led them into the arms of another.

So women are not exclusively emotional beings but actively need both emotional and sexual intimacy. Clearly, sexuality is far

What You Can Learn from Women Who Stray

The issues that factored into infidelity can best be summed up as:

Both emotional and sexual dissatisfaction in the marriage figured about the same: 44%

Emotional dissatisfaction in the marriage was the primary factor: 26%

Sexual dissatisfaction in the marriage was the primary factor: 7%

Other: 23%

more important to women than most people think. Both unhappy women and cheating women reported that their number one sexual issue was infrequency with unsatisfying sex coming in at a close second. I'll explore female sexuality and what my study uncovered in this area in chapter 7.

JANE'S STORY
I Wanted to Feel Passion in My Marriage

I worked hard during my marriage until I started having children. I made decent money, but my husband and I decided I would stay at home to take care of the children. It worked okay until we decided to sell the large house we lived in when the housing market was still a little strong and move our three children into a tiny temporary rental apartment until the housing market dropped enough for us to get the best deal on a new house. The rental was a very frustrating place to live because it was so small and I had a new baby and two other little ones.

I wanted so much to be a homemaker but found it impossible when we were only staying for a few months. We ended up renting much longer than anticipated because my husband refused to commit to buying a new home. We had the money, but the market was still dropping and he wanted to wait for the best deal. When he got home from work, I had to get out from the crying children and the home I hated. And since we weren't having sex, though I'm still not sure why, I would go out and play golf or bowl in a mixed league while my husband stayed home and watched television and surfed the Internet.

After spending so much time together with another man in these leagues, trouble just happened. We connected and he made me feel so desirable, beautiful, and sexy. I didn't leave my husband for another man, and I didn't have sex with the other man until later. I left my husband because another man made me feel something that was so lacking in my marriage that I couldn't bear the thought of going back to it and never feeling that way again. I would rather be alone and have the chance to feel that way than be trapped in a marriage to a person I know I'm never going to feel passionate about. I still see this man, but have dated other men as well.

Jane's story, like most I heard, spoke to the fact that women who have remained faithful or have cheated are quite dissatisfied in both their emotional and sexual lives at home. Many suffer quietly, feeling stuck and unable to make things better. There is a collective desperation to their tone, but this desperation can be resolved quickly with the information this book is about to explore.

Women Want More Time with Their Men

For the women who participated in my research, the number one emotional issue was not having enough time with their husbands, but feeling underappreciated followed closely behind. Lisa's and Tom's stories are similar to many stories I heard during my study: simply not spending time with your spouse will often have a severely negative impact.

LISA'S STORY
Time May Not Be on My Side

When our kids were small and I complained to my husband that we never spent time alone together, he'd always say that we'd have plenty of time for that when our kids were grown and out of the house. It was as though I was the bad one for even asking that we go out alone or take a vacation without the kids. Naturally, I didn't want to get away from my kids. I was a good mom. But his mom lived down the street and was more than willing to help us out. He just never wanted it.

That was my life for years. We both worked and came home and it was all about the kids. We had some sex just because we needed it, but that was something else we'd be able to do plenty when the kids were gone. It was like I was expected to wait about twenty-five years for time with my husband. I became like a sister to the nanny, to the point that I even took some trips with her and left my husband home with the kids and his mother. I probably would have just continued, but God showed me a different plan. At forty-one, I was diagnosed with breast cancer that had spread to the lymph nodes. Suddenly, waiting for a future time seemed stupid and I was mad at my husband. He probably got more anger than he deserved, but I promised myself that if I got through it, I wouldn't beg my husband for his time anymore.

By chance I ran into an old college friend and when we had dinner, I was astounded at how good it felt to actually be having time and attention from a man. We were practically strangers, so I was astonished that he was giving me a lot more in one meeting than my husband had for twenty years. It wasn't long before I just told him everything and he was there for me. We got sexually involved within a few months. I couldn't believe he could find me interesting and attractive with everything I was going through. My husband doesn't know, and frankly, my life is too complicated to change anything. At least through this horrible experience, I'm receiving some love I sorely miss, and I'm holding on to it until I'm stronger.

Top Emotional Issues for Women

My husband did not spend enough time with me: 20%

I felt underappreciated: 19%

When I shared my feelings and thoughts, my husband did not understand or address my concerns: 17%

Other aspects of my husband's life were more important to him than our relationship: 11%

My husband often lost his temper and was frequently moody or angry: 7%

We were no longer interested in the same things: 7%

TOM'S STORY
No Time for My Wife

Looking back, I was a real arrogant SOB. I don't have a good reason for it. I just thought that marriage was like that. I was at the top of my firm, lecturing nationwide, and was just really good at focusing on myself. I was good-looking and so was my wife. When she first got pregnant, I just shot out of there and found every reason to stay away. I had plenty of legitimate excuses to work late and I enjoyed being a workaholic. But I also went out late to some clubs, strip joints, whatever I wanted at the moment. I never cheated, at least nothing more than some mindless close drunk dancing and kissing.

I laughed at friends who were henpecked. I had it all. A

beautiful wife who respected my job, the money I brought in, the freedom I needed. She even agreed to bring another woman into our sexual play to satisfy my curiosity. She figured better that than have me stray. Then we stopped having sex for a while and I went to Hong Kong on business for about three months. When I returned, everything was different. My wife had seen a therapist, and for a long time I blamed the therapist for turning my wife against me.

I still did nothing, and then she told me she had seen a lawyer and was serving me with papers the next day. I went crazy. I was completely taken aback. I just stood there and began to cry, really cry. How crazy that it wasn't until that moment that I really wanted to save my marriage. My wife didn't get it. She assumed I knew it was coming and had already begun to play financial games to cheat her out of money. I don't know where I was. I just thought this was marriage. We go along until we don't, but I never thought she'd be the reason it stopped. I began to beg for another chance and agreed to go to the counselor, where I learned for the first time how much I had hurt my wife. She really felt like she wasn't attractive anymore or that I really didn't like her. It took her decision to divorce me to turn my head around and realize what a horrible husband I had been.

As I went through therapy, I made lots of changes and was able to become much more of a husband to her. She was skeptical every step of the way, but I was determined to spend the rest of my life with her and now I was really spending it with her and not everyone and everything but her.

Obviously a time investment is necessary to start a relationship. What we do with our time once we're in the relationship may change, but nothing happens without spending a proper amount of time. And here is perhaps the biggest difference between men and women as it relates to marital satisfaction. Men seem to be content with less time with their wives. What time means to a loving relationship for a man is miles apart from what it means for a woman. One woman summed it up best when she wrote to me, "When my husband spends time with me, that tells me he finds me attractive and lovable."

Women seek time with their husbands to connect with them and to feel they are an important part of their husbands' lives, whereas men do not even look at time with their wives; it's not really on their radar. Men are also looking for a way to connect with the women they love, but they factor time into that only as a practical tool. For example, for a man, sex is connecting, as is an appreciative comment, a hug, a thoughtful gesture—but time doesn't weigh into that. If the dinner, sex, and appreciative comment are all completed in thirty-five minutes total, he's good to go. For men, time is only a means to an end. For women, the time *is* the gesture. This doesn't mean that just sitting in the same room is all a woman needs. But even if she has a great thirty-five minutes, that doesn't mean she's done and wants to run off to do something else. Men are trained to accomplish tasks. Men go to work to get a job done much more than to put in time at the workplace. Men might have to stay a certain amount of time at work to collect a paycheck, but the goal is accomplishing objectives.

For men, time itself has little meaning except that certain amounts are needed to get things done. We don't use time to make a statement. Even if a dad takes his son to a ball game, how much time that takes is irrelevant compared to the action of seeing the game itself. Thus, if the home team is losing badly, the dad will probably leave early with the kid. He typically does not hang out until the end just because it's nice to spend time with his child. No, the task of seeing the game has been accomplished.

Women desire their partners' time in order to develop their relationships. They feel that no matter how many tasks have been completed, partners still need to spend time together regularly in order to feel close. On this topic, women are absolutely right, and not spending enough time is one of the most unfortunate mistakes men make. Men forget that life is not only about tasks. Love relationships involve much more than just completing tasks.

Children are a prime example. A man can make great money so his wife can stay at home and take care of the children. He can send his children to the best schools, give them the best camp and travel experiences, and yet be the most emotionally distant dad on the block. He can accomplish so much, but having a close relationship with his children will never be about anything other than putting in consistent time. He may be a really loving guy, but his children will not feel comfortable enough with him to share their truest feelings unless Dad is there for them consistently. A son may know Dad loves him and would do anything for him, but he still doesn't come to Dad with his emotional highs and lows, because Dad can't possibly get him. True understanding about what makes a child tick—what his dreams are, his fears, and his sense of purpose—cannot happen without time. Dad can't walk into his child's room and say, "Okay, we've got six minutes. Tell me about your dreams and aspirations." A child only reveals these deep thoughts when sitting around spending time with someone on a regular basis.

That's why children tend to share a great deal more with Mom. It's not necessarily because Mom is a better listener or has better responses. It starts with the basic fact that Mom values time as a message of love in and of itself. Time doesn't have to be about getting something done. Maybe moms are better listeners because they spend enough time truly understanding their children and then can respond to their children from being inside the loop instead of sounding like they don't get it. Children will share their deepest thoughts with someone they feel gets them. They also tend to share their biggest fears and concerns when things are calm and they're just hanging out with Mom. Commonly, a young child will ask the big questions when lying in bed next to his mom, who is just reading or spending quiet time with no other purpose than to show love by being next to her child. That's when she hears the really deep, hard questions, like "What happens when we die?"

Men do not see the correlation between spending time and creating a great marriage. They have difficulty readily seeing how having dinner together or reading side by side, discussing news events and laughing, is going to directly affect their lives. On the other hand, every hour a man spends working gives him a concrete sense of how useful that time was. After that time spent, he'll have fewer calls to make, will have finished the e-mail, will be closer to sending in the report, will have made more money working overtime. This allows him to measure his use of time in a way that he can't when spending it with his wife. Yes, men could measure the time they spent with their wives last night by whether they had sex. Again, a clear accomplishment—and an attitude that drives women mad because it looks like the reason he spent the time was to accomplish that objective. Most men are being nice not only for sex. Rather, they're always looking for a concrete measurement of success, and having sex is a pretty good one.

Men need to learn from all of the women in my study that the true measure of a relationship is the good feelings of being loved and loving another. It's not something anyone can just make happen with a single gesture. If a man buys his wife a beautiful present, he shouldn't be surprised that she's complaining just a few days later that he's not paying her enough attention (yet many

How Women and Men View Time Differently

- Women view time as a message in itself that they are valued.
- Men view time largely as a vehicle to accomplish tasks.
- Women prefer ongoing time spent with their husbands to big presents.
- Men use presents as a way of giving time, showing they've spent time by working to afford the present.

men seem shocked if this happens). One big gesture isn't going to do it. He wants her to understand how many hours it took him to work in order to make the money for that present. She wants him to understand that she'd rather have him to herself for all of that time he spent working to make the money for the present. That would be her most precious present.

For Women

Women often tell me they are disappointed when they suggest spending quiet time with their husbands, and their husbands act like it's some sort of big sacrifice. Men need to understand that your need for time is good for the relationship. Both of you are entitled to time together. Don't see your request for time as a pathetic bargaining chip that you must use to get your husband's attention. You don't have to feel belittled, or as if you're begging him to spend time with you. Ask him outright and explain to him why it's important to the two of you. "I'd like to spend more time together this week. I just want us to have some quiet time to chat and catch up, so we're feeling close. When is a good time for you to plan just thirty minutes or so a few times this week to spend pleasant time, have a drink, and relax together?"

But you need to understand that men see time as a vehicle to get things done. They don't value it as something to use to get closer to you. When you respect that men's minds work differently, you will find that understanding will help you to not take his behavior so personally; in turn it will be easier to discuss and manage it.

For Men

Keep in mind that your partner wanting time with you is a wonderful compliment. If she didn't like you, she'd be more than happy to see you go. Unfortunately, there are many marriages that exist in that paradigm. Remember how wonderful it felt when you fell in love. It was empowering and it made life different. That came from focusing time on your girlfriend, and yes, you accomplished something concrete: you got her to become your wife. But do not allow marriage to end your desire to be in love. Consider how great you feel when you wake up in the morning after a lovely night of fun and love with your wife, compared to waking up after a night full of fighting and acrimony.

Stop seeing time as a vehicle to accomplish a task. Time is necessary for your love relationship to be successful. When you spend time with your wife, it sends the message to her that you want to be connected to her and that you find her special because you'd rather be spending time with her than doing anything else. Be with her when you spend time. Get rid of distractions like the BlackBerry or the cell phone. Use the time to ask her questions about her day and share some of the more entertaining parts of yours. Set aside a certain block of time to be with her, with the understanding that you will accomplish being closer to her through this time spent. And do not keep asking her what time it is.

I've consulted with Fortune 500 companies, and one thing that every top manager knows is that if someone is going through a divorce or other intense stress at home, his work output is caput. Immediately, managers begin to rely less on that person and reduce his workload, and they aren't surprised when deadlines are missed. Love, or lack of it, affects every part of a man's life. Being in love may not feel as concrete to you as completing an e-mail, but make no mistake that it lies at the root of everything you do. Although Albert Einstein proved that time is not absolute—leave it to a man—time is absolutely necessary when "accomplishing" the "task" of love.

JEN'S STORY
He Was Wonderful When He Was Around

I cheated on my husband, Ben, a great guy whom I still love. It sounds horrible, and I'm writing this because I'm trying to figure it all out. From the beginning my husband was so loving and warm. He was all over me. He couldn't keep his hands off me and always complimented me. We played volleyball three nights a week on a local team and I couldn't believe how great everything was going. I was the proudest wife in the neighborhood. My friends were jealous. But a few years after we married he left his job to start his own business with his best friend. I think his friend really took advantage of him because it was my husband who was doing all the travel-ing and all the worrying.

At some point, I don't know exactly when, I just felt so lonely. I just missed Ben so much and I hadn't had sex in forever. He took trips that lasted a few weeks, and then he'd stop off at home and a week later, he was gone. I started working, even though I had a toddler, just to keep myself busy, and I cheated with my boss. He wasn't nearly as good-looking or as nice as my husband, and I knew it. But it was like I needed to be loved so badly.

My husband caught us when he surprised me by coming home a few days early. He was devastated and I understood. He was working so hard and I was doing this behind his back in his home. He couldn't forgive me, and frankly, I can't forgive myself. But I guess when I really let myself go there, I just say that as wrong as I was, I didn't get married to be alone most of my life. It's not like I told him he had to make a ton of money, so start your own business. He needed to do that to feel good himself and I went along with it. Maybe I shouldn't have. I just think it's our own little tragedy because we really were so good for each other and we have this absolutely wonderful little girl who has two fantastic, loving parents who didn't make their relationship work.

How Much Time Women Spend with Their Men

I asked women on average how much time they spend daily with their husbands alone talking. The number one answer for dissatisfied women was under thirty minutes per day. The significant news is that the number one answer for happy, faithful wives was over thirty minutes a day. More than twice the number of happy women reported spending more time with their husbands as compared to unhappy wives. Plus, 22 percent of the satisfied (faithful) women said they spend on average over sixty minutes per day talking or spending time alone with their husbands. Compare this to the dissatisfied women—just 5 percent reported spending this amount of time with their husbands. On the other side of the scale, about 23 percent of dissatisfied women reported spending less than five minutes daily with their husbands.

For Women

Creating time alone together with your partner is the most important thing you can do to make yourself happier and feel more in love. It's worth bringing it up to him and getting exact times that will work for both of you. Remind him that you miss him, you love the time you spend together, and you feel you two have to get back to being in love, and that the first step is just finding the time. Ask for thirty minute blocks of time a minimum of four times a week to start. Use the time to relax together, do fun things together (surf the Web, play Scrabble or other board games), and make it about pleasant conversation for both of you. Agree to put cell phones away during your time together.

For Men

If you want a happier mate, start by spending more time alone with her daily. Carving out this time is your best bet to create a better marriage. Go to your partner and suggest to her that you spend more time together. Make a plan for just thirty-minute blocks of time in the evening or whenever the two of you can be alone together. Name the nights you'll spend together each week, a minimum of four to start, and if you use a weekly calendar, refer to it to make sure nothing will conflict with this alone time. Now, consider how excited you are when you watch a sporting event, car commercial, fishing or financial show on television and compare that to how you feel when you spend time with your wife. Begin to see that you may be reserving all your enthusiasm for interests other than your wife, and that leads to a failed relationship. Consider how to make the time you spend with her loving and exciting.

Prioritizing Your Time

Later, we'll discuss how couples can really connect on an emotionally intimate level and stay actively in love. But first, it's crucial for a couple to decide to prioritize time together. I know that many men will read this and say, "Now I have to spend more time with my wife? As if I need another job!" And I don't mean to say men dislike their wives and would rather do anything else than spend time with them. If a man finds spending time with his wife a struggle, the next chapter will speak to changing that. But everyone has to realize some cold, hard facts. If you are working a typical 40-hour workweek for 50 weeks a year, you're up to 2,000 hours each year. If you spend 30 minutes per day together as a couple for 50 weeks a year, you're up to a measly 175 hours a year (350 hours if you get in a full hour a day). Keep in mind that many couples will spend more time together on the weekend rather than each weekday, so that figure of 30 to 60 minutes per day is based on a weekly average.

I find that women are quite clear that they do not expect their husbands to spend a ridiculous amount of time with them. Many men, though, do not understand how truly little time they are spending with their wives. An hour a day may sound like a lot, but when you think about everything else you do that you want to be a success at, it probably pales in comparison. If a man watches just two football games a week, that's almost eight hours, already more than the one hour of daily time that I've suggested he spend with his wife. And let's not forget the Saturday college games,

Monday Night Football, the added Sunday Night Football, and, yes, thanks for NFL Thursday nights as well. And consider the amount of energy and excitement you expend doing that, compared to when you are with your wife. It starts to make sense that women are feeling less and less valued by their husbands' time commitment.

Remember, creating time for each other is considered a gift, an act of love for your partner. You'd feel pretty crummy if you were always chasing after your wife trying to spend time with her, while she was finding many other "more important" things to do, especially if some of those things were watching a TV show or surfing the Web aimlessly. Women don't want to feel that they are always the ones talking about spending time. They don't want to be the only ones responsible for creating loving time together.

Some people say that they're so busy with work that they can't have additional pressure. Not a viable excuse. If work is such a pressure cooker that you can't be bothered to consider the so-called love of your life, then perhaps there is something wrong with work. Isn't work primarily a way to afford a lifestyle to be shared with your spouse and kids? Most hard workers look forward to some form of retirement because work in and of itself is not the end, but rather a means to an end. Yet what sense does it make if the means slowly destroys the end result of having a loving life with your family by not affording you time and space in your head for your spouse?

Consider honest change and understanding in this area. No one is expected to give up his day job. But nobody wants to feel that she is begging for attention either. Do you want a spouse who is a partner or not? If you want your love to truly share life with you, then be a partner in creating time, as well as sharing the pressures of your collective lives.

Substituting Time Instead of Creating It

You do not need to find a twenty-five-hour day to be with your partner. You probably need to reduce the time you spend doing other things that, when push comes to shove, are not necessary and not nearly as important as your love life. I am referring to hobby time, Internet time, favorite television shows, and work, which comes home more easily today in the form of e-mails and BlackBerrys than ever before. The Internet and television absorb enormous amounts of the average person's time, and these are the first places to review when wanting to find time to be with your partner.

Perhaps you do not enjoy the time you spend with your partner. Or worse yet, you find it uncomfortable. Perhaps you are confronted or criticized whenever you spend time together. This could likely be because you spend so little time together that there's an urge to confront everything you've been holding onto when you finally have the opportunity to sit quietly for a moment. If you both take the concrete step to spend time together daily, you'll see an immediate change. Perhaps the beginning will be awkward, stilted, or even uncomfortable, but that will quickly improve with your renewed focus.

Put aside your differences at the start. Fight the urge to make the time all about what has been going wrong. There will be plenty of time for that if your commitment to spending time together continues. Sometimes, when a woman wants to tell her husband about something he's done that upset her, she feels there's never a good time, so she will choose the worst time to express it, such as the first time they're finally spending some quiet time together. It's understandable. She feels that in order to enjoy her time with her husband, she needs to get this off her chest, have him understand what's upsetting her. For those women who feel this way, however, consider, "Will my goal be accomplished?" When you really think about it, you might realize that starting out with a criticism will not serve your purpose. The time you'll spend with your husband will be uncomfortable as each of you airs your grievances, causing you to have less time together in the near future and to be even more upset at each other. If you do want to bring up something critical, make it fast and be done with it. This moment of pleasant, relaxed time is hardly the setting to have a full-blown discussion about some pain that your husband caused.

Another problem is that many men, and women as well, can't stop talking about work. They're more than happy to fill the air about job-related issues. When the bulk of time is taken up with a monologue about work, it does not create a mood of friendly relaxation. A woman once told me that her husband cheats with fruits: his Apple and BlackBerry. Men, this BlackBerry addiction has got to stop. Put it away during your time with your wife. For many of us, the urge to touch that buzzing, ringing thing is just too strong. Spending time means having each other's undivided attention.

CAROL'S STORY
He's All about Work

Scott, my husband, couldn't talk about anything except his work. It was like he was obsessed, taken over by some alien being. When I married him, he was a pothead. We were fresh out of college, so it was okay and we had a lot of fun. I always knew he was hyper and that's why I was okay with his using some drinking or other things to calm himself. But when his father brought him into his business and Scott opened a new office where we lived, everything became about the business.

If we went out to eat at a restaurant, it was to see if it was a good place to take clients. If we vacationed, it was to check out the hotel for a conference. He has endless energy to talk about work and how we're building our nest egg. Our portfolio can get me hours of talk if I want. He's sliced and diced our bills over and over and down to the penny, we've been over our family "plan." But it's really just his plan to do nothing else but focus on money and work. I know those things are important and I'm glad he's working, but I need more.

Making Your Time Together Enjoyable

- Make appreciative comments about your spouse spending this time with you, even if you feel he or she should be doing it.

- Resist the urge to use time together to express pain or anger that you feel your partner caused you.

- Start by talking about something you think your partner will be interested in.

- Use your old "dating" techniques for making pleasant conversation.

- When you expect to spend time together, you'll naturally start thinking about the things that happen during your day to share later on.

- Remember that the better this time feels for both of you, the more motivation you will have to spend more time together.

Since we had difficulty having kids, we figured we'd take a few years off from worrying about it and I started working in his office. He really wanted me there, and I figured, if you can't beat 'em, join 'em. I thought at least I'd be a part of the office gossip and issues, and it would bring Scott and me closer. It did give us even more to talk about, but the focus on the business never ended. Everything else in our life is second to work, and it takes up every part of our lives together. He doesn't think about sex anymore. He'll do it with me if I initiate, and it's pretty nice, but I know that if we could just talk about business instead, he'd be just as happy.

I've become very close to a man who's a consultant in our firm. He's older and has been the only one to understand Scott's obsessive personality. He's even spoken to Scott about it. But Scott told me how disgusted he was that this consultant would turn to Scott's personal life. I don't know what to do. Recently, this guy and I started some kissing and it's gotten a little heavier. I told Scott I wanted to quit the business and focus on having kids. Scott got so angry, insisting that now isn't the time. I don't have the heart to tell him that staying in that office isn't going to be good for us. Scott is a really good guy underneath it all. All of his focus on money is just to secure good things for me and our eventual family. I'm holding on to myself, but I don't know what comes next.

When a couple decides to start spending time together daily, that is a gift of kindness and love. You want to be with your partner more than you want to do other things, and that means you love and value each other and find each other interesting and attractive. The only way to make the time together engaging and fun is to spend more and more time on making it so. If you just sit there and expect your partner to entertain you, I hope he or she has got a lot of material prepared. If you want to enjoy your time together, consider what will make it enjoyable for you. I'm not suggesting you sit at a table for an hour a night and expect to have so much fun or so much to talk about after the first few times. Consider what *you* bring to the table. When you were dating and getting this person to love you, I'll bet you had some ideas prepared for making your time together pleasant. I'll bet you spend some time on thinking about how to manage work or the kids. Your relationship deserves no less. Your partner might be more than happy to spend some of the time engaged in an activity that you enjoy, as long as it engages both of you.

Talk about what both of you like to do, and see what works for you. Perhaps you want to have a drink together and chat about your days, play backgammon as a backdrop for conversation, read to each other from that day's paper or a book you're currently enjoying. And naturally, there is nothing wrong with cuddling and offering a massage or something enjoyable to your mate with no agenda other than connecting emotionally.

Sadly, when couples don't spend time, they don't even think about what to tell each other from their day, which lends itself to gross detachment and a sense of independent living. Knowing that you're spending time together most nights, you'll begin to tag stuff in your head that you want to remember to share later, whether it's a fascinating news column, a funny event, a child-related issue, or troubling news at work. Now, not only are you spending time reconnecting at night, but you are also far less detached by day because you are stopping yourself to grab moments to share with your spouse. This is the attachment that successful couples develop, which is constantly building. The more we spend time, the more we remember stuff to share.

The more we share, the more we understand about our spouse. The more we understand about our spouse, the richer our experiences sharing with our spouse become. It just gets better and better. And it all begins with the commitment to finding regular time.

4

Appreciation = Value

I don't think anyone would be surprised to learn that women want to be appreciated. When I asked dissatisfied women what issues factored into their unhappiness, feeling unappreciated was the number two answer. Sadly, when I asked cheating women how the people with whom they cheated were different from their husbands, the number one response by a long shot was "made me feel appreciated."

In my research for my book *The Truth about Cheating*, one of the big surprises was that men said they felt grossly underappreciated. That seemed huge, because men seem very strong and capable and somehow we think that means there isn't a real need for appreciation. But most people are aware that women want to be appreciated. Many people feel this is due to their being weak or needy. That's a myth I'd like to destroy right now.

Women feel underappreciated because society in general doesn't recognize what they do nearly as much as it recognizes men's contributions. Men make money; and even if they don't make so much, everyone assumes that they are the primary wage earners. The house and all of its contents are readily seen by the naked eye, and it is assumed that these concrete, material things are due to the man's hard work and success.

Women get the short shrift in this area. Regardless of how much money they make or whether they are the primary bread-winners or contribute significantly in a financial way, society often judges them solely by looking at how they manage their homes, and their children if they are mothers. Society assigns mothers the brunt of the responsibility for caring for children, keeping them alive and healthy, buying them clothes, and making sure they do okay in school. Women's efforts in this area are hardly visible to the naked eye, and they are not acknowledged with much appreciation.

But the real strength of motherhood, of course, is invisible. It is the undying love for children that translates to a twenty-four-hour job of giving care and warmth to others. This love creates an internal imagery for a child that she will draw on for the rest of her life. Every decision and choice she makes as an adult will somehow whirl back to her early years, and she will maintain life's activities rooted in the messages and impulses from her childhood. But this is nothing you can *see*. Can we look at a kid and say how incredible his mom must be for him to have turned out this way? We can. But it's rare for a child to be all great without having some problems—and besides, who says it's his mom's doing and not the influence of his dad or a host of others who love him? It's this invisible role that has led too many husbands and even children to ask women, "What do you do all day?" Somehow, any answer seems to pale when compared to the man's assumed hard work that makes money and puts bread on the table.

This imbalance once led my wife, who stopped teaching at school to be a full-time homemaker and care for our five children, to respond creatively to a group of people who asked her what she did. She replied that she ran a home for needy children. She went further to outline her daily duties: clothing, feeding, cooking, caring for their educational needs and emotional well-being. She laughed at that point and explained that she was taking care of her own children. Everyone had a good laugh out of it, but she'd made a fascinating discovery: she was considered a saint if she was a mom to other kids, and just a regular person who received zero attention if she did the same for her own children. By contrast, a man gets credit for making money even if it's for his own family. So much for equality.

Even when a woman is working hard to make money for her family, society supposes that her husband is the primary breadwinner and largely responsible for the family's material well-being. It's assumed that her income helps pay for "extras"—private school, camps, vacations—not always considered essential to a child or a family. Even if her work helps to pay the electric bill, society is likely to assume it pays a smaller percentage of it. Simply put, society sees men as doing the main and crucial work, whereas it sees women as filling in the gaps. This unconscious perception can exist even if one is faced with facts to the contrary. If a woman is working hard and making significantly more money than her husband, it isn't something she can usually point to or take obvious pride in. People would tend to feel sympathy for the man and might even assume he feels devalued by her success. Women don't report hearing a great deal of praise for being capable and hardworking the way men do.

Hopefully, when we stop to consider this, we can clearly see the fallacy of this attitude. In fact, we know that you can throw a lot of money at a child and she can still grow up feeling lonely and insecure. It's not having a big house or expensive food that feeds a child's mind, heart, and soul. It is the love that is focused on her, and for this every parent deserves enormous credit. Women have long felt underappreciated because their hard work doesn't seem to get the same kudos measure for measure as the work of men. It has nothing to do with being weak or insecure, except that women unfortunately may feel this way because of the messages society generally sends. It's a shame, because the situation is easily remedied. Understanding the hard work that women do and showing appreciation are not difficult; they require simple mindfulness.

KATIE'S STORY
He Really Appreciates Me

My husband and I are both doctors. I was incensed when he started moping because I was chosen as chief of vascular surgery of the hospital where we both work. He's doesn't even do surgery much anymore due to a hand injury, but still I began to feel guilty. This was a great step up for both of us. It would eventually mean more money. Yet I received a phone call from his brother asking me to decline the job because it was too upsetting to my husband. I couldn't believe it. My husband said he never told his brother anything like that and his brother reached his own conclusions. My husband is a good person, and he was being honest in saying that it did really bother him. Due to his injury, his dreams would never

be realized, at least the professional ones. But he did understand he'd have to get over it and not mope, and he was very
happy for me individually. Still, my own mother advised me
to be careful not to throw it in his face, to play it down, and
not to tell anyone in front of my husband.

I was expecting a party from my family and friends, and
instead I got this. If my husband had gotten this promotion,
I would have been dancing for joy and throwing my arms
around him all the time. But not only did I not get appreciation for what it took for me, a woman in a man's world, to get
this far, I was made to feel guilty.

There was another doctor who ended up working for me
who thought I was unbelievable. He said all the right things
and meant them. He found it extremely sexy that I had
reached this position. Since he was a doctor in the same field,
he knew what an incredible accomplishment this was. This is
how my husband should've reacted. This man appreciated
every part of me, and the thing he loved about me was the
very thing that threatened my own husband. My husband still
doesn't know about my infidelity. He's feels he's being a good
husband just by not moping anymore. I need a lot more, and
this man means the world to me. He's the one I call now with
a problem as well as when I've had a great day or any other
success. In the last two years my husband and I have become
strangers. I feel like he wants me to become morose like him.
Unless he can be the best and brightest, our relationship
obviously doesn't work for him.

Learn to Value Your Partner

As human beings, we are drawn to one another. We literally cannot continue as a species without interacting. We will never be

whole, independent beings, but rather will always be like the pieces of a puzzle. How can anyone feel fully secure and confident if we are dependent on others? We're all in the same boat except that we live on a continuum of varying degrees of self-value. But there is no such thing as a person who does not need anything from someone else.

How we feel about our value is tied to how we are valued or devalued by those around us. Of course we want to feel good about ourselves without relying on the judgment of others, but how do we truly know we are good without being open to the opinions of those around us? From the day we are born, we are made aware of our parents' judgment of us, and that itself has a lifelong effect.

In our relationships, we must understand how important it is to both receive and offer this value. Without it, we devalue each other and make our relationship more about just getting the chores of life done. When one feels unappreciated by a partner, it gets translated into a devaluing message and potentially deadens one's spirit for love and warmth.

Let's face it. There is one person with whom we are most vulnerable, who shares our ups and downs and our challenges and triumphs: our mate. Living as an open book is daunting, because we are far from perfect and yet we want to be accepted. We want to believe that we are good in essence and generally doing the right thing. The world stands ready to judge us negatively as it suits each individual's agenda. Our mate is that one person who we desperately hope doesn't have a hidden agenda and just wants what is in our best interest.

Too often, however, husbands and wives don't trust each other. They've spent too much time criticizing each other and focusing on deficits and shortcomings. This often leads to an overwhelming amount of negativity and distance. Women like Katie in the

previous story begin to withhold information from their husbands, seeking to minimize their vulnerability. Quickly, emotional
distance sets in.

CAROLYN'S STORY
I Lost Myself and the Truth

I never felt like I was in love with my husband the way I
should be or wanted to be. He didn't appreciate who I was
from the very beginning. I married him because I was pregnant and had little going on in my life at the time. I was spin-
ning my wheels in a ditch, going nowhere. I'd always wanted
babies, and I knew he would love and care for me. He was
safe and reliable, and he would support me financially. His
father dropped a ridiculous amount of money in his lap on a
regular basis. My first baby was my first love. I had another
baby soon after, and I was living in a love fog. It was the happiest I'd ever been in my life.

I was so in love with my babies, so happy each day until my
husband came home. Becoming a mom allowed me to be
"me." But my husband didn't see the beauty in me as a mom
or the love I was giving. He couldn't share in that love with
me, and that's really a lot of who I was. He didn't like that
part of me. My husband still wanted the party girl in heels
with drink in hand ready to hit the sheets when he came
home. I did and I do love him as a person, but not like either
of us deserved.

Our marriage became bad. He began taking antidepres-
sants and drinking more, so I hated him more and raged
more. He was fine as long as we were having sex and he had
beer. He was not the father I wanted and needed him to be.
For some reason, I medicated myself with the kids. They

loved me and appreciated what I did for them. I had a third child, and life was good again for a while but then we started fighting. I have to say I was a terror, a raging bitch, full of anger, hate, and resentment. I hated myself and my husband.

When I began contact with the other guy and we became friends, I felt again. All it took was a nice guy liking me for who I was to make me realize I could wake up again.

When a friend of mine found three lumps in her breast and was given a death sentence, I let go of everything—all the *should*s and *what if*s. I started taking baby steps out of my marriage.

The Benefits of Appreciation

The number one answer cheating women gave when asked how the person with whom they had the affair differed from their husbands was "he made me feel appreciated."

- Women's contributions tend to be less appreciated than men's.

- When you appreciate, you send the message that you value your partner.

- Appreciation brings out the best in your partner.

- Appreciation sends the message that you've summed up your partner as good.

- Appreciation inspires your partner to continue doing what gets appreciated.

Appreciation Brings Out the Best
in Both of You

Appreciation is the way that we offer our partners the value they need. When I offer my appreciation of you, it sends the clearest message that what I see in you is good. I could choose a million things to say or do, but I have determined that the most substantive part that strikes me is the good in you or your effort to do something good. This has nothing to do with whether you should be doing this good thing anyway. Perhaps the most common obstacle to our offering appreciation is the idea that my partner is supposed to be doing what she is doing, so why appreciate it? Somehow if he is supposed to be making a good living and be a good dad, if she is supposed to be helping financially and be a good mom, then there is no appreciation for that. For far too many people, appreciation is reserved only for efforts that are above and beyond the call of duty.

Appreciation is a simple gesture that says what you do or have done is good and I'm thankful that you are doing it. It has nothing to do with whether the action is expected. I have always planned to make a good living and be a great parent, but I still want to hear from my wife that she recognizes how much effort goes into accomplishing these goals. And she deserves the same. Don't think of it as an extra goodie. Appreciation is not icing on the cake. It *is* the cake. *Appreciation increases your value and your partner's value.* It strikes at the very core of who you are and what your relationship is about.

Let's see the truth here. All of us have positives and negatives housed within our complicated systems. What brings the different parts of us out? We know that although we surely can't control our partners, we can do a great deal to affect how they'll behave. You can get your partner to smile right now. You know how. You also know how to really upset your partner. When you appreciate your partner, you send the message that you see the positive; and whether or not you notice the negative, you choose not to focus on it. This in turn brings out the best in that person. It's quite simple human behavior. The more we are appreciated for our goodness, the more we are naturally inspired to respond with positive behavior. Unfortunately, it also works in the opposite direction: the more you focus on your partner's negative sides, the more your partner will draw on that and act accordingly. It becomes a vital part of your collective relationship. Partners share their opinions of each other constantly, and those opinions weigh heavily on how the other partner chooses to respond.

Imagine it for yourself. You just got up at five-thirty in the morning to drive your child to a special school event. When you return, your spouse thanks you so much and adds that you're a really great parent. How does it feel? Good enough to do it again, right? Imagine if you came home to no comment at all, or were criticized for what you didn't do yesterday. It would leave you uninspired at best and angry at worst. How we act toward our partners really does have a great deal of impact on how they will feel and act.

I've always wondered why appreciation isn't given naturally more often. It's pretty simple and it costs nothing. But I've come to understand that it's really much more about judging our partners favorably. You can still sit down with your partner and discuss the changes you need to make and the business of the marriage, but always remember that you have the power to bring out the best in your partner. Develop this culture of appreciation and you'll immediately see a positive difference in your relationship.

You might need to explain to your spouse why appreciation is so crucial to you. Nobody should be demeaned because of a need to be appreciated. Sure there are people who have an unhealthy need for praise, but that's uncommon. Let your partner know why you require appreciation and why you are also going to focus on giving it much more as well. You may have to be the one to initiate it. When your partner visibly appreciates your appreciation, explain your desire to feel the way he or she is feeling just then. This way, you show your partner the feeling you want to receive, instead of just talking about it.

LORENA'S STORY
He Asks Me What I Do All Day

I have three children, one who has an autism-related disorder and two others who are also quite a handful. My husband works hard and makes a decent living. I'm in charge of everything. I do everything for the kids, pay the bills, clean the house. My husband would come home expecting dinner and a calm atmosphere. He'd actually say I'd put him in a bad mood because nothing was done when he arrived home. What he meant was he wasn't being served like a king. I was getting so angry that I was turning into someone I hated.

One night, after I had spent hours in the day combing through my autistic son's hair for nits, my husband was upset when I told him dinner wasn't happening and he said, "What do you do all day?" I threw a glass toward him and it shattered against the wall near him. He got angry, I burst into tears, and our children were scared. I stormed out of the house, and when I returned an hour later, he actually apologized. I'm not sure what happened, but my older daughter told me that during that hour he couldn't manage anything in the house and kept asking her to help him do everything. Maybe he realized what I do all day and night.

I can't tell you how everything changed when he said he was sorry and admitted that he'd been insensitive. Later that night we made love for the first time in forever. The next day he said he'd been like his father, and he remembered not liking it as a kid when his father put his mother down. He was doing the same thing and didn't want to do it anymore. Life is still crazy hectic, but just a little thank you from him now and then makes such a difference.

Create a Culture of Appreciation

I find appreciation so important that I can't reduce it to remembering to make a nice comment here and there, or a kind gesture when you happen to think of it. Both men and women need appreciation on a regular basis. Don't limit your appreciation only to actions taken by your partner. Appreciate the essence of your spouse. Make it a way of living—a new focus and a challenge—to draw out of your mate his or her goodness in response to your appreciation. Any goodness, kindness, warmth, giving, sacrifice, thoughtfulness can be focused on and appreciated. Use appreciation to cause you to act lovingly. Yes, of course, make appreciative comments and gestures, but use appreciation to really focus on the beauty of your partner's soul. Don't worry about what is not happening in your relationship, or how much you wish your partner could be better in many things. Guess what? Your partner has the same laundry list about you. You can always get to your problems in a discussion you set aside specifically for that purpose, but the best way to elicit more of what you love about your spouse is to focus on the good by letting your spouse know how much you adore and appreciate those qualities.

A culture of appreciation changes people by lifting them up and giving them value. Appreciation comes in all shapes and sizes. A simple comment that verbalizes clearly what you appreciate is always welcome. But there are simple gestures that also can say how much you are focused on appreciating your partner. A hug or kiss connected with an appreciative comment goes a long way. A small present, a thoughtful poem, or a greeting card all say that you are thinking of your spouse. Appreciation does not have to be about a single event, like "Thanks so much for making dinner." It can be a general summation of your partner's personality: "Thanks for being you," "I love how kind you are," "You're so beautiful inside and out," all come under the category of appreciation. Sometimes men report that they feel that expressions or gestures aren't "masculine" or "who they are." It's important for men to allow themselves to become comfortable with being this appreciative person and to understand how much the women in their lives need it. It's possible to think about their own need for appreciation and then be open enough to try the following activity:

1. Create a long list of things you love about your partner.

2. Each of you create a list of ways you'd like your partner to show you appreciation. Give your lists to each other.

3. Once a day, show appreciation using one of the ways your partner wrote he or she would like to be appreciated.

4. After one week, begin to show appreciation twice a day so that it becomes the norm for you.

Women Want Men Who Get the Household Thing

My father-in-law never changed a diaper. I've changed over five thousand of them. Probably double that, really. My friends are all hands-on dads. But some of them think of it as "helping," whereas others view it as a partnership with the woman they love. Women want to feel together with men who desire to share life, not find ways out of participating. Your life as a couple should be happening together, and this includes collaborating around the house, whether cooking, cleaning, changing diapers, or hiring someone to help with household chores. There is no one way to take part in household tasks. It is about a mind-set and a feeling given to women that they are not alone. As my wife used to tell me, "There's nothing sexier than a man who does dishes." When men and women accomplish tasks, even menial ones, as a unit, it significantly increases the emotional connection between them. When men choose not to participate, or do so grudgingly, women hear a resounding message of disconnect from them.

For Women

Tell your partner what you'd like from him. Perhaps he "should" know, but trust me, there's some biological difference so that when a man hears "clear the table," he does not take it to mean that everything should be off the table. He just doesn't. He thinks it means get the stuff that could spoil off the table, get the stuff that needs washing off the table, or get almost everything off the table. What may be obvious to you is not obvious to him. Do household tasks together so that they're not individual chores. This way you can be in the same room, perhaps talking as you both clean or cook. Finally, find some space for the two of you that is exclusive of the children.

For Men

Don't "help" your mate. Be a true partner and live life as a unit. Recognize the pleasure in maintaining your lives together. If you aren't focused on the laundry and you ruin it, or you forget the baby in the store, why are you surprised when your wife is angry and feeling distant? Get in there together with her. You can follow a recipe—cook and freeze some meals one day. If she's sick, that's the time to be there with food and medicine. Hire a cleaning service so she doesn't have to worry about the house. Gather the laundry and send it out if you don't want to do it yourself.

Don't do these things grudgingly. This is a way to show your love that she'll remember, and it means so much more than anything you can buy. A family friend, a rabbi of fifty-some years, recalled that when he was a young man, his new bride was once in bed with a cold. He noticed that she was sad. He asked what was wrong and she said, "Nothing." He asked again, and finally she told him that she knew it was silly but when she'd lived at home and was ill, her mother had always fluffed up the pillows and made sure she had water. He told her she wasn't being silly at all. He fluffed the pillows and brought her water, and they grew together into a beautiful marriage of over half a century.

LISA'S STORY
My Husband Doesn't Appreciate Me

I've spent my life trying to do the right thing. I know I probably have a problem not liking myself enough, but my husband definitely added to it. We met in college so we've really grown up together. For years I did what I thought was the right thing. I quit my job to be a full-time mom. Now I know that was a bad idea, but I thought that was the right thing to do and my husband wanted it as well. I probably did it because he wanted it. I just wanted to please him and it just seemed like I never could. I read cookbooks, for God's sake, and all I ever heard were little jokes about thank goodness we have money to go out and eat a lot. Everything was a little jab, a joke, and it was always about me. My driving, my cooking, my lack of knowledge about the financial world. I was an art major, so I knew a lot more than him in that area, but that didn't count.

It was at my fifteenth high school reunion that I hooked up with my old boyfriend, the first boy I had ever had sex with. He said hello, and I just knew we were going to reconnect. He was unhappily married and had recently separated from his wife. It was all wrong that he was so interested in me. He was fascinated by my art knowledge and how I'd been such a good mom. When he looked at me and seemed to think I was doing the right thing, it was like a drug. I had to have more and more.

When I returned home, I knew that I had to do something or else this would all end in disaster. If this old boyfriend had lived around the corner, I doubt there'd be any question what I'd have done. I asked my husband to come to therapy with me and I couldn't believe he agreed. It took me all night one night to rehearse asking him because I was so nervous. When the therapist asked me why we were there, my husband looked to me to get started since I had asked for the meeting. I just burst into tears and yelled out, "He doesn't like me." I could see the genuine shock on my husband's face. He couldn't believe I felt this way, and claimed it was the farthest thing from the truth. He was scared I was going to ask him for a divorce because he felt I had been distant for a while and didn't know why.

We've kept our therapy going. Each of us has our own therapist and we also meet with mine for couple's therapy. It hasn't been easy, but I think we're slowly figuring things out and we're both learning to show how much we like each other.

. . .

When you fail to appreciate your partner, you're not only taking him or her for granted but it's perceived that you don't consider your partner valuable. If you're not feeling appreciated, explain this to your partner to try to help both of you cure this part of your lives so you can both become inspired through a newfound culture of appreciation.

5

Understanding Does Wonders

It is one of the top problems that faithful, unhappy women have with their husbands; and it is the second most common reason that unfaithful women say they have cheated on their husbands, not far behind number one: "When I share my feelings or thoughts, my husband either does not understand me, does not address my issue, or is not willing to talk about it further." When faithful women were asked in my study how their husbands could improve the relationship, the most common answer (58 percent) was "be willing to talk to me more about my thoughts and feelings."

BETTY'S STORY
A Wave of the Hand

I was convinced that only gay men truly understand women. At least that's what my husband used to always say. He was wrong. My ex-brother-in-law did a great job. When he divorced my husband's sister, we had a lot in common to discuss about the failure of our marriages and our spouses' inability to really love. They were both raised by a cold, mean mother, so I'm sure that had something to do with it. I know I don't sound too guilt-ridden. As I write this I have to confess I feel bad, of course, but I don't know what my husband expected. He never had time for my opinions or anything bothering me. He had time for sports and kids' activities, but my thoughts were met with a wave of the hand like it was some magic wand that made them go away. I think he would've been thrilled for me to have as many girlfriends as I needed to do what he should have been doing, talking to me about what was on my mind.

The straw that broke the camel's back was when I was going to tell him that Marvin, our ex-in-law, had made a pass at me. Can you believe that I was nervous that he'd be mad, so I started with something pathetic like, "Honey, I have something really bothering me," and he chuckled and said something about my period coming. That was his getaway plan. If I ever "had" to talk, he told me to take a Midol and call him in the morning.

It wasn't funny the morning I called him to let him know the service processor was bringing him the divorce papers. I was steaming. I had one child and she was out of the house so I wanted to move in and start a life with Marvin. That's where I am now. The biggest problem has been that my daughter is angry at me and my (soon-to-be-ex) husband has milked it for everything he can. We'll get through it. I know that now because I am with someone who truly listens and loves to hear me and my thoughts. I can't tell you how good it feels after all these years.

Women and Anger

Many women in my study indicated that the pained frustration of not being heard, and being made to feel unimportant by their husbands' lack of interest in trying to understand them, led them to feel angry.

There could be many reasons that a woman might feel anger. Whether it is from feeling underappreciated, unheard, or sexually frustrated, anger is a major indicator of how your relationship is faring. Note the extreme disparity in how many women are angry a lot among the different groups, as shown in the chart on this page. Women who cheat or remain faithful but have considered

Satisfied Women Are Not That Angry

	Unfaithful	*Faithful (dissatisfied)*	*Faithful (satisfied)*
A lot	54%	68%	14%
Sometimes	30%	29%	44%
Hardly	8%	0%	30%
Not at all	8%	3%	7%

separation or divorce in the last year are angry a lot. In the faith-ful group, 68 percent of women who are dissatisfied are angry a lot, compared to only 14 percent of the faithful women who are satisfied in their relationships. Clearly, if you are a woman who finds yourself angry at your husband a lot, or you are a man who finds your wife angry at you a lot, your relationship is likely in a very bad place just from that fact alone. It is a bright red flag that the relationship needs some immediate positive attention.

Interestingly, being angry a lot is not a cheating signal, as you can clearly see. Dissatisfied faithful women had a higher rate of anger than cheaters (and cheaters talked about how angry they were *before* they began cheating). It is much more a clear indica-tor of relationship damage and the need for changes. Each part-ner must recognize the danger of either cheating or a sad and failed marriage if the woman is angry at her husband on a regu-lar basis.

Consistent anger always needs to be explored. Unfortunately, many people prefer avoidance. As bad as the anger is, dealing with it seems an even more daunting task for couples. Anger doesn't go away because we pretend it isn't happening. It doesn't go away because we tell our partner to stop being so angry. Yes, anyone can request that a partner not *act* on that anger in inappropriate ways, but that doesn't mean the partner isn't going to be angry, just that the anger will be quieter. There are people who have anger con-trol problems, but they tend to rationalize their behavior by say-ing their partners are driving them crazy, making it difficult to assess the problem.

I always suggest that the angry person immediately become determined to change any inappropriate angry behavior. Again, the women in my research said they were angry a lot, but that doesn't mean that they voiced it in an unhealthy way. But if you are initiating and *regularly* making biting comments, screaming, cursing, or even throwing or breaking objects in fits of rage, you need to take responsibility for this unhealthy behavior. What typically helps a partner to do that is the understanding that the other partner is finally willing to sit down and seriously consider what is so upsetting and what can be done about it.

As I explain to the "silent" partner, the fact that your mate is so angry and acting out doesn't mean that he or she doesn't have a valid point. It's just that the point gets lost in the anger, enabling you to turn away and invalidate everything because the anger looks so bad. If you truly want the anger to go away, do your part in resolving the underlying issues. Commit to new behaviors, and see what happens. If the anger is still seriously present, it gives you the opportunity to look at and force your partner to take responsibility for the anger. After all, you'll say, I've made such significant changes and we are committed to a better path and you're still very angry. Anger may be a problem you need to look into personally.

Both partners must do their part when there is anger. Doing nothing will very likely lead to cheating or dissatisfaction in your marriage. Women want their anger to be taken seriously. They want a "sit up and take notice" reaction from men without having to resort to screaming. When men respect the idea that women are angry and treat the anger as an opportunity to resolve something, or apologize without sarcasm or excuses, often women's anger dissipates. Nobody wants to be angry all the time. Finding the source of what is creating the anger is something a couple must do together if there is love in the relationship. Work together to reduce these sources, whether it be lack of sleep, demands of the job and parenthood, the toxic people in our lives—anything that is contributing to anger. Women want support, love, and respect, not condescension and indifference in the face of anger.

Often, it is the man's lack of attempts to understand his wife that can cause such a sense of frustration and insignificance that it quickly leads to her being angry internally. As we move forward, we'll explore how men and women are different in this area of understanding and what you can do to bridge the gap.

Men and Women Process Communication Differently

There is little doubt that if we wanted to find *the* major difference between how men and women work, communication would be the one. Many couples have difficulty communicating because men and women process communication differently, but there are some simple ways to make major changes.

Men and women approach conversation in a similar way to how they approach time. For men, conversation is a vehicle, a means to attaining a solution and completing a task. Men want to put a problem in a concrete package with a beginning and an end. For women, conversation *is* the solution. Often it is the genuine sense of having her partner understand her feelings in and of itself that brings the resolution. Both sides are looking for a similar end, but women don't feel the need to rush toward completion. The completion comes through the process of sharing and connecting.

We're not fully sure how much women's and men's different DNA influences the way they approach things. But we know that men, for instance, are taught to control as much of their environment as possible. This is why playing sports works so well for boys: there's a well-defined winner and loser. Moms clap on the sidelines with an attitude that "win or lose, it's how you play the game," and while dads acknowledge this, they may add with a wink, "It sure feels great to win, doesn't it?" Men are taught to have an edge, get ahead, and be the best. Men want to control so they can win, whatever that means to them. They have a solution-oriented approach to life; all processing is directed toward doing things better. Conversation is used to get ahead, figure it out, put something new into motion, or come up with a plan. Naturally, a man feels that he only needs to discuss a given topic with someone he thinks has particular knowledge and experience with the issue he's trying to solve.

For this reason, many men do not share their thoughts and feelings with their wives. If it's a cognitive issue—a work problem or financial problem—men will often think that their wives lack the education or experience to truly understand and offer solid advice. Even if it's a personal success, a man is more likely to share it with a colleague, who can really understand how hard it was to accomplish the task, than with his wife, who'll be happy but, he thinks, cannot really understand what effort went into it. Of course, much of the time the reason she can't understand it all is that he's been unwilling to share information about it regularly. If a man has an emotional issue, such as sadness over a parent's illness or fear that he's not a good enough father, he'll likely avoid the entire topic with anyone because there is no concrete "solution" available and thus it's better to swallow hard and sweep it way under the rug. Maybe he'll discuss the situation with another man who's been in the same boat, because he'll understand and perhaps share the knowledge he gained from his experience.

I was fascinated when I learned about a certain business organization that offered group experiences for people to discuss any business or personal issue. It had a very rigid rule that no one could give advice. In fact, no one could try to "feel out" the situation the other person was experiencing. You could only respond if you'd had a very similar experience, and then you could only share what had happened to you and what you had done about it. The person discussing the problem could then choose to use that information to help decide how to solve his problem. I'm not judging the idea, as it does prevent people who share from manipulating or being domineering in their opinions on what the other person should do. But imagine how limiting it is, how distancing to not try to plug into the other person's feelings regardless of whether you've been in the same spot. The sharing of experience is a highly valued male characteristic, especially when the purpose of the sharing is to solve a problem. The man wants to hear what happened to someone else so he can decide what should happen to himself. This pattern offers a concrete end and the illusion of control.

Women see things quite differently. Women are not taught the same need to find a solution, so they are not looking to have one conversation as short as possible so that they can determine what to do and put it into action. Does this sound like any woman you know? Also, again putting aside the possible influence of DNA, women are taught to feel for others. They are taught to feel for the one who loses, to have empathy for people and animals in general. Society often still sees women this way. Women are not looking to get the edge, to get ahead in the same way as men. They have a more "Can't everybody have everything?" attitude. If we see mothers who hunt for pleasure or competitive mothers who are only happy if their child is the best, it makes us uncomfortable. We don't feel the same way about fathers who have these traits. A father wants his child to be happy, but it's fine if he sometimes wants his child to be "better" than the next kid.

When it comes to conversation, women are not looking for hard-nosed advice that they can kick around and come up with an immediate solution and put their issue to rest. They're not looking for a concrete task to be done. They want to feel that someone can feel their feelings, can take part in sharing their emotional issue. That in and of itself is resolving the issue for them. The processing of feelings is what gives women a sense of calm in the midst of turmoil. Women have been given the right by society to focus on most of their feelings. They're allowed to cry, express that they are emotionally hurt, and be physically demonstrative without any negative associations. So for many years women have been allowed and therefore given much experience with being in touch with their feelings and have no need to rush through and be done with them in the same way that men have.

Men have been taught to stop crying and take the pain so that the ten-year-old boy in the middle of a sports game, for example, can get back up and be ready for the next play. This becomes a metaphor for his life. Avoid pain, but when it strikes, take it, get through it by putting it aside as soon as possible, and move on. This attitude has its advantages, but being a connected conversationalist isn't one of them.

Men and women have their work cut out for them to be able to find a happy medium. Unfortunately, as we see from my research, many couples are not doing a very good job of it. The first part of building a better communicative style is to understand why the two of you are so different. Otherwise, as it usually happens, each partner takes the situation very personally. She feels he doesn't care and value her and that's why he's not sharing or listening. He feels she's badgering and getting angry at him instead of respecting his wishes to not talk; in fact, much of the times he literally doesn't know how.

Yes, this may be amazing to women, but I have spoken to many men about talking with their wives, and they respond by telling me, "I don't know what I'm supposed to say." One woman wrote to me through this study, "After two years of therapy, my husband has learned to say, 'I understand,' and 'I'm sorry,' without having any real understanding or genuine apology attached to it. My dog seems to understand me much more than my husband." Understanding how both of you come to this aspect of life so differently can give you the renewed patience and energy you need to work on your communication with each other. The next section will outline some techniques to help you with this important part of your relationship.

SUZANNE'S STORY
Undiluted Attention with No Cell Phone Interruption

"It was the courting and the undiluted attention that started to feel like a fix, like a charge. I wasn't even aware it was fully happening. You're feeling creative; someone's listening to you." Suzanne explains the feelings that led her to consider an affair with the designer helping her decorate her house. "There were meetings over lunch, stops at the coffee shop, and there were no cell phones. My husband was attentive too, but I shared him with his job and his kids from his first marriage, and I never really thought about it.

"Here was an unattached person whose job was me and my thoughts. I hired Allen on the recommendation of a friend, and before I knew it I found myself attracted to him. The project took over us, and I wasn't even aware. I've seen it happen to friends who get involved in political campaigns or other projects that invite passion. Pretty soon you and the other person are sharing a great deal. My husband, Jim, was just like, 'Uh huh, right, okay do what you think, honey,' and he seemed to find it intrusive when I asked him to work through a decision I had to make."

Suzanne had married Jim, a man in his sixties, while in her mid-forties, after dating a string of men who could not commit. "He wasn't exciting, and that was okay. I didn't think I was missing anything. The truth is, I'm not a high-maintenance person. I don't need a lot in the way of physical or emotional attention. And what we had was always good enough. Once in a while in the bedroom, not a lot, which was okay by me. And lots of evenings out, always with friends. But ultimately I didn't have the affair, because I knew what would happen. You lurch into this affair and you have to think about if you want this total upheaval in your life. I just didn't have the certainty that what I would have with Allen would be better than what I have with Jim. Aside from the moral problem of breaking the vow I made to Jim, the reality of following the quick fix, to get the rush from the affair wasn't worth it. I would jeopardize a whole structure and I'm smart enough to know that for Allen it wouldn't be about the future. The complications weren't worth it basically. Hurting Jim, messing up what we have . . . Well, who am I going to really have to share my life with, this new guy?

Fortunately I just didn't start something I wouldn't be able to stop. I was able to look at the bigger picture and see it all for what it was. I knew that if I went forward, someone was going to get hurt and ultimately it would probably be me. Looking down the corridor, I saw myself with Jim and it helped me to make the better choice. Losing the attention and rush was a sacrifice, but I was able to acknowledge that the bigger sacrifice would be my future when it all fell apart."

How Women Can Help Men
Listen and Share

First and foremost, keep in mind that having the time to be together, as we already have discussed, is the most important prerequisite in good listening and communication. When couples have time together regularly, they can't help but be filled with conversation. The more consistent time there is, the greater the framework within which they can build those skills naturally. Here are a few of the most important techniques to help you on your way.

Women need to outline what they want from their husbands. If you do this effectively, chances are you will not have to do it for the rest of your life, although you might have to remind your husband from time to time in any given conversation. Start off the conversation by saying something like, "I have an issue I want to share with you. I don't want you to feel like you have to give me advice. In fact, I'm not looking for that. I just want to know that you can understand why I feel the way I do. Please just understand it from my perspective. Forget about you and what you'd do or how you'd feel. I'm not looking to make a decision about it right now."

Women are often frustrated when their husbands seem to take the side of the person that they are complaining about. It would be helpful for them to understand why. Men are problem solvers. When he takes the other person's side, he wants to show you that person's perspective so that there can be negotiation and some solution. He is afraid that if he "takes your side" and understands your feelings, this will make you even angrier and cause you to strike out somehow against that person. If the other person is someone from his family, he is even more inclined to divert you from your anger and show you that person's point of view. It's likely that if he were sharing a difficult situation with you, he'd be looking for a similar approach: a suggestion about what the other person is thinking so he could make a balanced decision about what to do about that person's actions.

This is, of course, the exact opposite of what most women want to hear from their husbands. Men often do not understand that women feel good when their husbands understand, feel, and agree with their perspective. It doesn't make them angrier. It has the opposite effect. They no longer need to be upset, because just sharing the load with someone they love in and of itself diminishes the energy of the feeling.

Women are not going to think, "Well if my husband sees it the same way then I'll really take aggressive action." Often, men do feel this way. If a man shares with his wife that he's been mistreated or his feelings have been hurt, he thinks it's his manly role to get aggressive or else his wife will see him as a weakling. Women need to check themselves and see if they're sending out this vibe. When a man shares something with his wife and she wants him to be more emotional about it, she can send that message more effectively by reassuring him that it won't make him look weak to her by saying something like, "I really want to know what it felt like for you."

When you are about to share your feelings with your husband, tell him as best you can what you want from him. Reassure him that his comments will not cause you to do anything drastic, and that most of all you are not looking for *him* to take action (unless that *is* what you're looking for). Men think they are supposed to solve the problem for you either by giving you the best answer or by taking matters into their own hands. They love taking matters into their own hands because that gives them the most control under any circumstance.

Also, set a time limit on your conversation. I know that women do not want to feel like they're on the clock when sharing their personal thoughts and feelings, but most men are terrified that the sharing will have no end. Remember that because men are unaccustomed to listening and sharing on this level, for some of them it is literally exhausting. Many men would rather run a marathon than spend an hour being emotionally and conversationally attentive. Over time, that will change for you and your husband as you develop this part of your relationship. But in the beginning, giving him a start and finish time will help motivate him to stay attentive and engaged.

His knowing that in about twenty minutes, let's say, the conversation will end no matter where the two of you are will help him be with you on this journey. I'm not suggesting a clock be placed on the table, but just the idea will give him the comfort that you understand it'll end soon, and he'll be able to focus. You may object to this suggestion and feel that he's not a little boy and you deserve more than that. Yes, you do. I only make the suggestion to help you as a couple develop this emotional part of your relationship. It's not much different than when I suggest couples put a time limit on a meeting to discussing family finances. In that case many men may go on and on discussing money and budgets, but many women can focus more on the meeting if they know it'll have a predetermined end.

When your twenty minutes are up but you have more to say, agree to table the discussion for now and take it up again the next time you're together uninterrupted, which hopefully won't be more than a day or two away. Also, let him know that just sharing these feelings with him has been helpful and his ability to just listen and get it is all you want. Let him know that you enjoy a loving, understanding response and nothing more, and that you may need to bring something up multiple times.

To get him to share more, explain to him why you want him to. Tell him you want to listen to what's going on with him. Outline for him what you'd like to hear about: his day, work gossip, conversations with family or friends. Again, the setting is crucial to the success of this part of your relationship. If it's difficult for men to share in the first place, then it's impossible for them to do so with kids interrupting, phones ringing, their stomachs grumbling, and the television blaring. It requires some sense of calm and togetherness, and having space to focus.

For Women: Getting Men to Understand and Talk

- When sharing your feelings, tell your husband what you're looking for: his understanding of how *you* feel under those circumstances. Tell him you are not looking for solutions from him and you will not get more worked up if he understands your hurt regarding someone else. On the contrary, it'll have a calming effect on you.

- Outline how he should listen: suggest that he ask you more questions and try to verbalize to you how he understands your feelings.

- Set up a time limit to this part of the conversation so he knows there's an end.

- Tell him you may need to share the same points again with him because you need the repetition to deal with things. Let him know that you want the same loving, understanding response each time you discuss the issue.

- Ask him to share just so you can understand him. Let him know you won't make suggestions or expect him to follow them unless he requests them.

- When responding with a feeling word, put terms like "a bit," "kind of," and "sort of" in front of the word.

When a man does share, stay away from using charged emotional language. Women are looking to extract the feeling part of a situation, but many men do not even allow themselves to feel the emotion associated with the situation, so they feel that women are not with them in the conversation. Plus, men are not naturally given to using emotional words and phrases, so they'll not likely enjoy a heavy load of it.

If he says about his colleague of twenty years, "Jim got fired today," and you respond with, "How very very sad for you," he'll probably shut down. He might give you that "Are you an alien?" look. He likely hasn't allowed himself to consider how sad he is; and if he has, he will not tip his hand and look all weak and mushy. Yet if you say something like, "Yeah, I suppose it's a bit sad," he might respond, "Sure, after all those years putting his life into the business and you know, he's just starting to pay for college for the kids . . ." Simply adding words or phrases like "a bit," "kinda," "sort of," before you mention any word having to do with emotions gives the man the opportunity to answer without feeling or appearing weak. He can respond positively because men do have feelings, of course; they're just not as comfortable experiencing and expressing them. A less intense approach will give him the opportunity he needs to speak from the heart.

How Men Can Listen and Share

As discussed, it's most important to understand how men and women are different in this area of their lives. So if you are a man and your wife just pointed you to this page, please read "Men and Women Process Communication Differently" on page 80 and then return here.

When your wife shares her thoughts or feelings with you,

simply ask follow-up questions. Don't try to come up with the solution, don't be in a hurry to get to the bottom line and move on. Find out what happened next, ask for more description of the situation: how she felt at any point or why she thinks the other person acted that way, for example. This will help you focus on what your wife is sharing with you and will keep you further away from trying to interpret it through your personal perspective.

Don't try to consider how you would feel if this happened to you. It's not about you. The fact that you might have felt completely differently has nothing to do with how someone else should feel. You might have had a different upbringing, might be less intimidated, might be a more anxious person than your wife. There's a variety of reasons that you might have processed the situation differently, but that's not what your wife is asking you to share. She wants only for you to know how she felt in that situation. The feeling of knowing how our partner is experiencing something is what makes us connected. There's no growth in saying how you would feel, compared to the growth of letting yourself experience how she feels.

You don't have to agree with her feeling or believe it's best that she felt that way. Perhaps you wish she felt differently. But that doesn't really matter. You won't convince her now to have felt differently at the time. And it's wrong for you to judge that her feeling was somehow not the right one. Perhaps how she chose to behave based on her emotion is something you could judge, but she's not asking you to do so. If your wife gets mad at your child, it's your job to understand her and let her know that you can see how she got to that point. And you can even understand it if she screamed. This doesn't mean you think her screaming was good, justified, or the best way of managing the situation. But she knows that. Discuss with her how the two of you could together develop a lifestyle at home that would help her not get to that point. It's not your job to judge, just to help.

You can fully understand your wife's feelings and experience and still wish for a different outcome. But remember, she is the love of your life, and when you try to see the best in her, the best will come out. Leave judgment out of this and save the solution or desire for change for much later. Just focus on understanding how it felt to be her in the situation she was in, for better or worse.

Next, acknowledge verbally that you understand her. Just say things like "Whoa, I can imagine it being embarrassing," "You were upset, no?" "Your friend should know better," "It must've felt wonderful hearing that." Let her know that you get the point and that you understand her feelings around the situation. If you get it wrong, she'll comfortably correct you or slightly adjust your understanding: Something like "No, it wasn't embarrassing in as much as it was hurtful." Simply be a part of the conversation in this way. That's primarily all she wants from you: to understand how she feels.

Don't give advice. Respect your wife enough to know that she can troubleshoot and consider solutions on her own. Sure, you may be able to help her in this way, but wait until she's asked you to do so. Don't ever skip the first step of fully understanding her. Imagine if someone began to give you advice and you thought he didn't get your problem at all. His advice wouldn't carry much weight. One of the mistakes men tend to make is believing that another man understands how he feels because he's been in similar situations. But you know that two men in the same situation can have two completely different perspectives, feelings, and outcomes. Really assessing a listener's understanding of you should be a prerequisite for taking advice. Your wife may not be looking for your advice, and if she is, she's looking for it only after she hears that you understand her.

Don't take the other person's point of view. Your wife is smart enough to know that the other person has his or her perspective. When you point out the other person's point of view, you send the message to your wife that you are working much harder to understand the other person than you are to understand her. You won't lose anything by being "one" with your wife and making her feel understood by you. Again, you can always dissuade her from taking an action you feel is not in her or the family's best interest, but that is only after you have given her the clear feeling that you understand her. By understanding your wife's feelings, you will actually reduce their intensity, because she will have gotten them off her chest and shared them. She no longer has to feel so strongly. Your understanding won't charge her up. It is much more likely to calm her down. You can clearly ask that she not make any decisions that involve you or your family of origin without asking for your opinion in the future.

Now consider how much you share with your wife. Do you wait for her to find you and get you to tell about your day? Seek her out instead of waiting. Tell her about your interests and concerns. Consistent sharing gives her the understanding about you that you ultimately want. You don't want to grow apart, or to feel that she doesn't focus on you or get you. Do your part regularly to draw her a map of what's going on with you. Get her feedback on anything that might be troubling you. Maybe in the past you didn't want to focus on your feelings, but using her as your sounding board to consider your emotions only brings you closer and helps you to better understand yourself. Finally, make sure you ask your wife to share her feelings as well. Some men only have the capacity to share or talk about what they have on their minds, and when that runs out, suddenly the tank is empty and they have no space to inquire how their wife's day went. Be sure to keep tabs on your wife's concerns and life events so that you remain connected as a couple.

For Men: Listening and Sharing

When your wife is sharing with you:

- Ask follow-up questions.
- Consider how she felt in that situation, not how you would've felt.
- Understand her without making any judgment.
- Verbally acknowledge that you understand her.
- Realize that you can understand your wife's feelings and still disagree with how she chose to act.
- Take time regularly to share your day with your wife.
- Discuss work-related politics, topics of interest, and news in addition to work details.
- Learn to be okay with hearing your wife's emotional word usage (angry, hurt, happy, thrilled) when responding to you. Take the time to consider with her how you did feel under those circumstances.

FABIONA'S STORY
I Liked How He Listened

I knew I wasn't going to cheat on my husband because the man I was getting close to was my gay business partner, Matt. I was becoming more and more attracted to him, and it started because I loved the way he listened and understood me. My husband doesn't seem interested in most of what I say. He's interested for a few minutes in my stories if he wants sex. That much he knows. He has to give me a little attention before sex. But it doesn't feel good. When Matt listens, he really loves to hear my thoughts and stories. It's just so wonderful to have a man who wants to know all about you.

I don't know what to do. I'm afraid if I don't stop it with my partner, I'll resent my husband more and more. But I've come to depend on my partner for validation and making me feel important and excellent at what I do. Matt always has time to talk and have fun. I feel young with him. He notices my clothes and my efforts to look good. My husband is fixated on his e-mail and sports. I sit and wonder if this is all there is.

MARGIE'S STORY
His Family Was Everything, I Was Nothing

It's ironic that when I married my husband, part of what I loved was his family. I was an only child and my mom passed away when I was a teenager, so having his parents and eight siblings take me in was huge for me. Little did I know that I was marrying the family. We bought a house within a block of everyone else. Every weekend was planned around the family, meals, events, birthday parties. It was great for my daughters because they have twenty-four first cousins, almost all of them living near us. But it became impossible when I couldn't tell my husband the smallest thing about being in any way unhappy with the family.

It was like there was this code of honor that the family had that no in-law will infiltrate and dare break everyone apart. When my husband and three of his siblings had a business, I wasn't allowed to ask why one brother was building another story and a pool onto his home while I was being told we didn't have enough money to send our daughters to private school. I couldn't question why my mother-in-law made all the deposits for the office and why she was paid an enormous salary when I was looking for a part-time job for a while to help us make ends meet.

Anytime I broached the family subject, I was given no time at all. And keep in mind that between the business and the kids, our whole life was all about his family. I'd hear from him when his sister thought I was rude and I had to apologize. I heard about how my daughter had to share her birthday with her cousin even if my daughter wanted one time to have her own party because her cousin was three years younger and received all of the attention. I even heard that I needed to stay away from the guy I eventually cheated with because my mother-in-law didn't like the way he was looking at me. He was a contractor and had done work in lots of my husband's family's homes, and we hired him for some simple updating, painting, creating two separate bedrooms for our girls out of one.

It was like he became the only man outside this entire web for me to talk to. I literally thought I was going crazy. My husband questioned my agenda so much, I really felt I was beginning to turn into a devil woman until this man came into my life. Since he had done a lot of work in the other family homes, he really understood how crazy it all was. He got how my mother-in-law worked and her favoritism and questioned why some children had an open checkbook and I didn't. He really listened and could understand it all. I planned to leave my husband, but when I told him, he told me the books will show he's made no money for years and that they'll all sue Craig, the contractor. I agreed to stay, really for the sake of my daughters. He's forbidden me to have anything to do with Craig, but I still spend time with him all the time. In a way I think I'm hoping my husband will find out and kick me out so I can finally get free of all this.

Be Willing to Go Where You Haven't Gone Before

Obviously, the purpose of listening and sharing in better ways is not to feign interest. It is to help each of us learn to have better focus on the important things in life, namely, the love of our life. When we live a loving life, we go to places we never anticipated. Imagine if your child is hearing-impaired, or becomes a brilliant violinist. You'd become an expert on either issue (or whatever is important to your child). Who would've believed that you would know so much about the hearing-impaired or the world of violin? But life takes us places, and we can either drag our feet or celebrate the twists and turns that open for us. Loving your partner means recognizing that you will learn and listen to things you never thought you'd care about. Because it is important to your partner, it needs to become important to you so that the two of you can grow together.

Too often, husbands or wives think that as long as they let their spouses do what they want and don't get in the way, everything will be great. And although no two people are supposed to live inseparably, there is great harm in accepting the concept that each of you will have different passions that will hardly ever be shared. In a relationship, we look to bring passions together so we see the vivaciousness in our partner and get in on that excitement. If something doesn't interest you, maybe it doesn't *yet*, until you find out more and learn more about it. We want to come close to each other, and allowing our partner to live life separately in areas that he or she is excited about seems very far from ideal. When you committed to your partner, you decided that what was interesting to that person would become interesting to you.

Research shows that couples in love have similar brain patterns. It's not a coincidence. They literally affect each other's thinking. Since they got in on the ground floor and have spent years learning about what excites the other, they have years under their belt of experiencing and growing their passions together. This significantly reduces the chance of either one of them ever waking up one day feeling distant and lost from the other.

Finally, let's understand that conversation and sharing don't always have feeling words in them. In fact, most of the time they don't. Many women think that unless real, raw emotion is being discussed, there's been no conversation. Not true. Clearly, most conversations have a great deal of emotion attached to them whether or not either person recognizes it. How we feel about a political or religious subject will likely tell the other person a great deal about us even if no feeling words entered the conversation. When men discuss world events, they are sharing an intimate part of themselves, and that should be seen as talking and conversation as well. One woman told me that she and her husband rarely talk, and her husband was astounded because as retirees, they spent their days together and he felt all they did was talk. She explained that their days were not filled with emotional conversation. She wanted to be talking about feelings. But most people don't sustain conversation strictly about emotions for very long. We can share feelings about issues, but sharing a lot about a very personal issue is challenging and draining. Yes, we want our partner to share on that level, but it is uncommon to have those conversations with such regularity. When we talk about politics, the family we met in the mall, and yes, your mother, we are actively engaged in emotional conversations that reveal a great deal of who we are. Use all your time together to connect over any topic, ask follow-up questions and relax the need to have consistent, long talks about profound personal feelings.

Simply put, be interested in what each of you has to say. Just saying the three words "Tell me more" will let your partner know that you care more about listening than about anything else right now. That's a very loving message.

REBECCA'S STORY
I Wanted a Man Who Shared Feelings

Rebecca and Peter were high school sweethearts, both brought up in very strict religious households. After Peter returned from World War II, they married and started a family, as was expected. The involvement with their respective families was stifling the young couple and hampering their ability to establish their own household. They decided they wanted space for themselves and education, so they moved to Europe, and using their benefits from the GI bill, they each earned a doctorate and set up a consulting firm.

"For a while we were very happy," Rebecca says. "But we were both brought up in difficult circumstances and it was a bigger trick to get to a different place psychologically than it was physically, so to speak. Both of us had parents who were immigrants with a volatile parenting style. Even though you promise yourself you'll do things differently, you hear your mother's voice come out of you when you have that first child, and those parental influences are very strong. Our own parents fought and we found ourselves fighting. We tried to change our styles and we explored psychological ideas and other interesting ways of changing things but, you know, even though we loved each other it was hard."

Peter had mood swings and what would now be diagnosed as posttraumatic stress disorder from his experiences in combat. He was given to silences and emotional withdrawal when angry. Additionally he had a hard time admitting he was wrong, not unusual for that generation. All of this made Rebecca feel isolated and, after one difficult argument, Peter refused to speak to her. This silence continued, making her feel increasingly alone and sad.

"One day, I don't know exactly why, I had just had enough. Because I'm action-oriented, I packed my bags, took the three kids, and left. I went back to the States. That was it for me. I wasn't sure what I would do, but I knew I couldn't keep living like this. I found a job teaching and a place to live. We stayed with a good friend while I did all of this, and her brother Nathan had always liked me and he came around a lot. He was single and sweet, with none of the troubles that my husband had. He was uncomplicated and I enjoyed talking to him. He listened and was very open and respectful, complimenting the good job I did caring for the children and remarking on my cooking. I could also tell he had feelings for me.

"What can I say? I was flattered. But I was also brought up in a religious environment and I believed it was a sin for a married woman to love another. I certainly wasn't going to give in to feelings. But it did occur to me as time went on, just to get to know Nathan a little more. What could be the harm? He asked would I like to take a walk, get out of the house a little. Sure, I thought. So we went for a walk and he told me this and that. It was so nice to be with someone easy, someone who talked about how he felt, which a lot of fellows didn't do. Men are different, I knew, but still, here was one who showed his feelings. He asked if he could take me out to eat.

"I knew Nathan was well-intentioned. He wanted to have a real relationship and so forth. I was alone, I had crossed an ocean and left my husband, but starting something with Nathan would have been a bigger ocean to cross. In the end Peter came over from Europe, he told me he loved me and asked me to come back. Whereas in the past I might have swallowed my feelings, I told him exactly how things had to be now. No more silent treatment, no more explosions. We would have to go see a marriage counselor. He agreed to that, which was unusual for the time. The feelings I had for Peter were complicated and I knew going to Nathan would never allow me to get anywhere with my husband. It would have made a complicated situation a complete mess. I think about Nathan sometimes and know in my heart I saved myself incredible pain by not starting anything with him. My husband and I did get help, and although it was a rocky road, we have had great moments of love."

Both sharing yourselves and listening to each other are so crucial to building a healthy connection; it's worth making sure you create a lifestyle to support this behavior. Ask yourselves if there's enough understanding between you and do everything you can to create more understanding, using the tips in this chapter. Understanding is the key to your loving connection.

6

Women and Sex

Let's put some myths to rest. The number one sexual issue for both the faithful women and the cheating women in my study was infrequency, with unsatisfying sex a close second. The problem of a man asking for too much sex was quite low on the list of complaints. Putting to rest the myth that women aren't "into" sex is my finding that the happy woman has sex twice as often per month as the dissatisfied woman. Clearly, when love is working for a woman, sexuality is a healthy and frequent part of that love.

ELIZABETH'S STORY
Waiting for Sex

When my husband and I exchanged vows in September 1999, I would never have dreamed that I would be the one to break them. After all, my husband managed different musicians—touring with major rock bands—if anyone were to cheat, wouldn't it be him?

Our problems started early on in our relationship, but my need to be in a relationship blinded me to them. We started dating in December 1993. A month into our relationship, we still hadn't gotten intimate. I assumed he would try to sleep with me on the first date. But as time passed, I was the one who ended up having to make the first move, which wasn't welcomed with the sparks it should have been that early on in the game. But I trudged on.

I had always been a pretty sexual person. I probably shared my bed with more people than I should have during my twenties and thirties. I chalked up my promiscuity to the fact that I was independent, I was in the entertainment business, and no one got hurt during any of my escapades. I never had a one-night stand with a stranger. Most of the people I slept with were—and still are—friends of mine. Some would come into play later in my life after I was married. I have no regrets about my past, but often regret my present.

As far as sex goes with my (now) husband, the first two years of our relationship we'd have sex maybe once a week, but it never escalated beyond that. Red flags, anyone? Nope. I didn't see them. Again, I was a twenty-nine-year-old single woman living in New York, and I was just happy to have someone around who took me to dinner, owned a house, had a great yard for my dog to run around in, and kept me company. My mother was happy, too. She felt safe knowing that I had someone, and I fell gently into the arms of that safety net, where I've been for eleven years now.

Around the third year of our relationship, the sex stopped completely. I was now living with my husband and we fell into that familiar pattern most people fall into after being together for awhile. At first I figured it was the fact that he was on the road a lot, we were apart, I was working a lot— I had a thousand excuses for the celibacy. Never once did I think he "just didn't want to have sex." As the months rolled on, I finally confronted him. He got very defensive, and I tried never to bring it up again. I just figured it would work itself out.

Probably the most humiliating moment came when I followed the advice of an article I read. "Buy some nice lingerie! Light some candles! Cook him a nice dinner! Bake a hot apple pie! He'll have you in bed before the steak hits the table!!" So I set the scene for a nice night of *Cosmopolitan* romance. He came home from a rehearsal, the house was dim, the smell of dinner cooking wafted in from the kitchen. I met him at the door wearing a beautiful peach and lace camisole and panties I had bought from Victoria's Secret earlier that day. I felt really pretty. And I was so excited to experience the night ahead.

That excitement came crashing down with the first words out of his mouth, "What are you *wearing*?!?"

"What do you mean?" I asked.

"You look ridiculous. Put some clothes on."

Even writing this, I remember the pain that shot through me with his words. Of course, it was plain as day now. I was not attractive to him. I looked "ridiculous." Never have I felt so naked as I did standing in the doorway that night, in my "ridiculous" panties, begging my husband to notice me and love me.

I ran into the bedroom, stripped off the clothes, put on some sweatpants, got out a pair of scissors, and in front of him, cut up the lingerie into tiny little pieces. I threw them at him, tears pouring down my cheeks. I never again tried to initiate sex. Over the years I would occasionally ask, "Are we going to have sex . . . ever?" He'd answer, "Yes, I promise we will. Soon."

We have had sex once in the past ten years. It was the night of a friend's Thanksgiving dinner. We each had a few glasses of wine to drink that night, and with love in the air, we felt a little frisky. We actually made out at several stoplights on the way home. It was fun. We came home, had great sex, and . . . that was that.

I feel like such an idiot even writing this. I should have been out long ago. But it's that safety net again. And hope. I've always hoped that things would change, that eventually he'd muster up the passion to want to be with me. So I waited.

That is, until about five years ago, when the seed was planted for my first affair. There would eventually be five in all. I chose to have affairs for two simple reasons: One, I was horny. Plain and simple. I wanted and needed sex. And two, I was hungry for love and attention. If my husband wasn't going to give it to me, I would find it somewhere else.

My girlfriends knew about our relationship. They urged me—on more than one occasion—to leave, but I just couldn't. I didn't know how, nor do I know how to today. My friend had a party and a beautiful guy stood across the room. He had gorgeous eyes that at one point met mine and . . . it was over. We talked for hours.

I pulled my friend aside and said, "Your friend Craig is *so* cute!"

She replied, "He told me he wants your number."

I asked her if she'd told him that I was married. She had. She'd also told him that my relationship was less than perfect and that if he was really into it, he should pursue it. She knew it would do me good and—as bad as it sounds—was hoping it would bring a little action into my life.

We went out on a few dates. The chemistry was insane. Though we spent a couple of intimate evenings together, he was reluctant to sleep with me because I was married. I have to give the guy credit for that. He didn't want to sleep with another man's wife. All I wanted to do was sleep with him, so we were overwhelmed by tension and—well—the relationship ended as quickly as it began.

It would be another two years until my next tryst.

I was back in my hometown for a job interview. An ex-boyfriend (who I will always think of as the love of my life) and I got together for drinks. The following night, he and a group of friends and former coworkers had a little party at his house. Drinks were flowing. The old stories were being told. And that familiarity reared its head, leaving the two of us in bed at the end of the night, right where we had left off years before. We had sex. It was great. I left the next morning feeling a little guilt, but mostly anger that my husband drove me to this place. His inattentiveness forced me to have an affair. I hated the place I was in, and so wanted to feel the passion I had felt that night for my husband again. But it wasn't happening, so I just dealt with it the best way that I could.

In January 2005, I started what would be my big affair. A full-blown, several times a week, think I fell in love, lasted a year and a half kind of relationship.

We met at work. I'll call him Paul. He was a really nice guy who I was attracted to immediately. I think that the feeling was mutual. We were talking one day shortly after meeting and he asked me if I had a boyfriend. I told him that I was married. Apologetically, he said, "Oh, sorry." And I said, "But it's not what you think." I proceeded to tell him that my husband and I hadn't slept together in several years. He told me about a girlfriend he had who lived in another state, thousands of miles away. She had children from a previous relationship. Though they had been together for—I think—about four years at the time, their relationship was getting strained because of distance and he was trying to decide what to do with it. He was super frustrated because his sex life had dwindled to about once every three months.

It didn't take long for us to formulate what we thought was a brilliant plan. "Let's have sex—nothing else—no commitment, no relationship . . . pure sex. It will help both of our relationships out." Wow—sounded good at the time. Wasn't it Seinfeld who said it could never be done? Seinfeld was right.

Within a couple of months we were having sex several times a week. Sometimes at night after work, sometimes during the day at lunch—sometimes at the office in the stairwell or in a bathroom that wasn't often used. We couldn't stay away from one another. I was crazy about him. I would have left my husband for him if he would have asked. But he didn't. And that was the beginning of the end for us.

He had decided—after a year and a half—that we should end our relationship. He wanted to concentrate on his (still) girlfriend out of state. Even if it didn't work out between them, the guilt that he was having over our relationship was killing him. He felt like he was betraying her, her children, my husband, and me. It was eating him alive. I never shared his guilt, which made me feel like a bit of a sociopath. I mean, how can I have an affair and not feel anything toward my husband?

When our affair ended, I was crushed. I didn't want to do anything anymore, including staying in my marriage. So one night when my husband was on the road, I just blurted it out. "I've been sleeping with Paul for a year and a half." He went from not believing me, to basically not caring. He never brought it up again. When he got back from his road trip, I brought it up again, thinking we should probably discuss it in person, but he just kept saying, "I know you wouldn't do that . . . I don't believe you."

And that's where it stands now. I came clean, admitted the affair to my husband, and . . . he just let it go. Pretty much like he has let everything else in our marriage go. I never told him about the others I hooked up with along the way, including a Brazilian ex who stayed at our house while my husband was out of town. What good would it do to tell him?

I don't know where our relationship will go from here. I don't know if I'll have another affair. I'd like to believe that my husband will eventually muster up some passion for me and tell me how much he wants to be with me. What's that? I'm dreaming? Maybe so. But I'm not ready to leave yet. And until I am, I'll just be patient and hope that someday things will change.

Elizabeth's story highlights some of the common issues that women reported in my research:

1. Sex is crucial. Having a solid emotional relationship with a man that is largely devoid of sex is a recipe for sadness and disaster.

2. Many women hold on to hope far beyond what the writing on the wall is clearly telling them. Elizabeth is still living with the hope that one day her husband will sexually satisfy her when there are years of history proving quite the opposite. Her sit-and-wait attitude will never produce a better sexual relationship.

3. She doesn't know what to do. She was deeply hurt when she tried the lingerie thing, and decided never to try anything again. She's right that dressing sexy is not going to get her husband's libido jump-started, but she's wrong if she thinks things will be corrected by doing nothing. Whether she chooses therapy, asks his best friend to talk to him, demands he see a urologist, or seeks separation, she has to do something if she wants things to change. Sheer hope just won't make it happen.

4. Elizabeth has blamed her cheating on her husband. Since he "drove me to it," she feels little or no guilt. Not to diminish her pain and struggle, but she'd be better off accepting control of her actions so that she could choose to change them. Again, divorce is a real option, or open talk with her husband where he understands her future intentions if he chooses to do nothing about his lack of sexuality with her.

Sex Is Important to Women

When I destroyed the myth in *The Truth about Cheating* that cheating men were not primarily motivated by sexual dissatisfaction in their marriage, it was assumed that it would be no different for women. And indeed, just like the small fraction (8 percent) of male cheaters who felt that sexual dissatisfaction at home was the primary contributor to their infidelity, only 7 percent of cheating women in my studies said the same.

Women's Top Sexual Issues with Their Mates

	Faithful (Unhappy) Women	Cheating Women
Sex with my husband is too infrequent	25%	27%
Sex with my husband is unsatisfying	19%	26%
My husband demands too much sex	10%	11%

However, the number one answer given by men when asked to sum up the primary reason they cheated was emotional dissatisfaction—well ahead of the next answer, which gave equal weight to emotional and sexual dissatisfaction. Surely, conventional thinking would be that women would overwhelmingly respond that their primary reason for cheating was emotional dissatisfaction. But conventional thinking is wrong. The number one answer by far (44 percent of unfaithful women) was that sexual and emotional dissatisfaction in their marriage figured about the same in their decision to cheat. Compare that to 26 percent who said it was primarily emotional dissatisfaction that led to their cheating.

You also might be surprised at some of the similarities between cheating women and faithful women. For instance, you might assume that women who cheat are more interested in sex than women who remain faithful are. But as we will see, that would be a false assumption.

Faithful, Happily Married Women Have Much More Sex

I asked women to report on average how often they have sex per month. For the cheaters, I asked how often they had been having sex with their husbands per month for the three months prior to the affair. Here's how they responded:

Cheating women: Four times per month

Faithful women who were dissatisfied with their marriages: Five times per month

Faithful women who were satisfied with their marriage: Ten times per month

Satisfied wives are having sex more than twice as often as women who are unhappy in their marriages. We can't conclude that just having more sex is the answer. Perhaps they're having much more sex because they're more connected emotionally. We can conclude rather loudly, however, that a happily married woman is having much more sex; and chances are, having more sex is, in some part, contributing to her happiness. So throw out your assumptions that women don't want sex, and if you're a woman, stop feeling any shyness about wanting to have better and more frequent sex. It's pretty clear that the idea that women are just not into sex is a myth.

When asked what issues contributed to their sexual dissatisfaction, women provided percentage values (adding up to 100 percent) for all issues that applied to their situation, so some women had more than one response. The top-rated issue for sexually dissatisfied women (25 percent) was that sex was too infrequent, while the runner-up (19 percent) was that sex with their husbands was unsatisfying. A much more minor issue (10 percent) was that their husbands "demand too much sex or make other sexual requests I'm uncomfortable with."

Cheating women reported similar sexual issues. The top two problems for them were that sex with their husbands was generally too infrequent (27 percent) and sex with their husbands was unsatisfying (26 percent). Compare this with 11 percent whose answer was that their husbands demanded too much sex. The pattern is clear. Women who are unhappy in their marriages realize that having more and better sex, along with fixing the other important emotional issues we've discussed, creates a much better, safer loving relationship.

PATRICIA'S STORY
We Put Lovemaking at the Top of Our List

My husband and I were in our early twenties when we married, so sex was never an issue in the beginning. But a few years later when we had our first babies—twins—wow, I was like a different person. I now realize I had postpartum depression; it was months of real hell. I didn't feel sexual at all, but I would have sex with my husband now and then, because I felt bad for him. After a while, he sat with me and talked with me in the sweetest way. He wanted to know how to help me feel better. I knew he also wanted to get back to our sex life, but he was cute about it. We talked about getting away and made it happen. It helped that his older sister, who's single and loves our kids, lives ten minutes away and could babysit. We went away one time just for one night when the twins were almost a year old, and it really made a big difference. I didn't know how much worrying about the babies or just feeling like Mommy sucked the sexuality out of me.

We decided that we were going to be committed to our sex life, and ever since then we've made it a point to make love on certain weekend nights, no matter how tired we are. Some nights it's great. Most nights it's not fireworks but it really makes us laugh when we have little energy but manage it anyway. We hear friends complain that they don't have sex much anymore and we tell them what we do. Also, my husband and I are really nice to each other. He always thinks of me and plans romantic surprises. I really feel like he thinks I'm great, and there's nothing sexier for me than my husband telling me how great I am.

Trust and Vulnerability in Sex

There are some clear physiological differences in how men and women achieve orgasm that I'll outline later in this chapter, but there is less information on the arousal process. What makes men and women aroused, and is there a difference? The Toronto psychologist and sexuality researcher Meredith Chivers, PhD, has begun the effort to better understand these differences. There are two points from her findings that are important to our discussion here. The first is based on a study in which she scientifically measured the arousal levels of men and women while showing them various video images of sexual acts. Every thirty seconds, a question popped up on the viewer's screen: "How sexually aroused do you feel right now?" The viewer chose a number from a keypad.

One of the most fascinating discoveries of the study was that the men answered in ways that corresponded to the scientific measure of their arousal, but women did not. In some instances, they said they were not that aroused, when the measurement of their bodies indicated that they were. Sometimes they reported being more aroused than their bodies indicated. Clearly, the women's minds were not as connected with their sexual arousal as the men's minds were.

Part of the reason for the difference may be that women are sometimes uncomfortable exploring what turns them on because of how it may be judged by others. Men are more comfortable sexually exploring and saying what makes them feel aroused without fearing the same judgment. Perhaps the women in this study were answering as they thought they were supposed to answer, or worse yet, were truly not in touch with their bodies. Some women have been conditioned socially to ignore or hide from their truest sexual desires, so much so that they really cannot pinpoint in their minds what is going on in their bodies. They are likely to be more capable than men of hiding from a feeling of arousal and not allowing it to register. Men obviously have a more difficult time hiding from arousal, as an erection gives it away, and they are possibly more conditioned to allow stimuli to turn them on.

Some women are more in the dark about their bodies and far less able to completely relax with their sexuality. This is definitely reinforced by society, which puts women into an asexual box. Women are supposed to be dainty people who are the mothers of the world, nestling little babies in their arms for a lifetime. How does that image mesh with loving sex and wanting to let loose sexually? Society has a special anger toward women (like the celebrities sometimes caught on film) who party while their children are seemingly neglected, while men who behave similarly are not judged so harshly. The idea of being a highly sexual woman is not seen as compatible with being a righteous or a maternal woman, presenting a dilemma for many women who may not even realize, as seen in this study, that they are being hampered in some way from being in touch with their own sexuality.

How does a woman begin to get around this? Dr. Chivers has observed: "One of the things I think about is the dyad formed by men and women. Certainly women are very sexual and have the capacity to be even more sexual than men, but one possibility is that instead of it being a go-out-and-get-it kind of sexuality, it's more of a reactive process. If you have this dyad, and one part is pumped full of testosterone, is more interested in risk taking, is probably a bit more aggressive, you've got a very strong motivational force. It wouldn't make sense to have another similar force. You need something complimentary. And I've often thought that there is something really powerful for women's sexuality about being desired. That receptivity element. At some point I'd love to do a study that would look at that. We just don't know much about it right now." It may be politically incorrect to say women are "receptors" sexually, but I don't believe that is her point.

Here we have perhaps the most important emotional understanding about male and female sexuality. Women can be very sexual beings, but to get there they have to be more *vulnerable* than men. Women have to allow themselves permission to feel arousal wherever it may come from and use it to be sexually active with their partner. Men do so with far more ease. How can women get to this point? That's where husbands can do a great deal to help.

Women in my study kept writing about wanting to be desired, but not with just a simple sexual desire, not as just a receptacle for the man's "needs." (You may remember the laughs we had on *Oprah* over Oprah's use of the term "sperm toilet," which one woman in my last study had used to express her feelings of disgust over how she felt she was being treated.) Women said they wanted their husbands to be overwhelmed by who they were as women, to see every part of them as special and alluring. They knew that in order to have great sex, they needed to feel great trust. For women there is great vulnerability in sexuality. Besides the fact that society has made women into sex objects to be used instead of respected, women are looking to sexuality as a supreme form of connection. There is a give-it-all-away sense of themselves when having and truly enjoying their sexuality.

There is a place in loving sex where we become lost. We are no longer sure where we begin and end. We allow ourselves a pleasure and feeling of rawness that can only happen in a very safe environment. It puts us all in a position of weakness because we will lose control and things will happen whenever our bodies want without our minds deciding when and how. This freedom is the ultimate beauty and satisfaction of sex, and the reason it draws us so close to our partners during this process. But for this kind of sex to happen, there must be two people on the same page who are completely trusting and vulnerable with each other.

Clearly female sexuality is anything but a solely sexual process. It is really about a woman's trust with her partner to let herself be consumed by her desires and use that process as a way to become much closer to the man. How can any women allow that when her husband just yelled at her, or will likely do so in the next few days, or put her down, ignore her emotional needs, be unwilling to explore her own sexuality along with her? The answer is that she can't.

All of us are very careful about our vulnerability, as well we should be. We shouldn't be throwing it around without the certainty that we can trust the one we are vulnerable around. Otherwise we risk getting very hurt. Some women told me they didn't want to be that vulnerable with their partners, and so they found their truest openness to sexuality a journey best left to themselves. Sex with their husbands was just sex and they didn't feel comfortable enough with them to really let themselves go.

For a woman to allow herself to become a happy sexual being with her husband, she'll need to trust him. She'll need to allow herself to get lost with him, and she knows she'll feel much more connected to him as a result. Her feelings will change as she allows herself to be more and more connected through lovemaking. Her mind and body will likely avoid lovemaking if she's concerned that the closeness and vulnerability that come with it are unsafe for her emotionally. If a man is sarcastic and rude, thoughtless and angry, he needs to work on himself before he can even hope to have a good sexual relationship (more on this in chapter 10). No woman should ever feel compelled to engage in sex with someone who doesn't make her feel good about herself. There is nothing real in that sexuality.

Women seem to be able to "turn off" or, as Dr. Chivers's study suggested, to ignore impulses better than men can. This was shown by both the dissatisfied faithful women and the cheating women in my study, who reported that they were having sex far less than those women who were satisfied in their marriages. But women also have sexual needs and can engage in the sex act for the sake of doing it, just as men can. The difference here is that this sex won't lead to a closer relationship, and inside her mind, she'll likely not be anywhere in the room. As more than one

Understanding Female Vulnerability during Sex

- Great, consistent sex begins with trust.
- There is a huge amount of vulnerability for a woman during and after sex.
- Lovemaking will make a couple closer.
- Women won't let themselves be "free" sexually if they fear emotional distance from their man during or after sex.
- Women want to be desired.

woman told me in the study, "I can have sex with him but I don't let him kiss me on the lips and look into my eyes. That's way too intimate." Sex can be reduced to simple satisfaction of physical arousal, but that does not make any couple closer with each other.

Really great, loving sex for any couple is about love, trust, and vulnerability. When both of you understand this, you can begin the journey to a much better sexual relationship.

GINA'S STORY
He Touched Me in a Way My Husband Never Did

My husband never told me how beautiful I was. I couldn't remember him telling me I was sexy or anything like that. I worked out four times a week without fail, and I thought I was decent but figured that I must not be, because he really didn't give me the time of day. He wanted sex once a week, got his fill, and that was it. I really hadn't had much sexual experience before marrying him, and the sex I had was kind of the same. It felt kind of nice until he was finished, and that was it.

The guy I cheated with made me come alive. He stroked my body, every bit with his hands. He was so incredibly gentle. I'd never had an orgasm, wasn't even sure what it was, until this man would not go on until I had one. That first time was so amazing that I just felt I had shared something with this man that I'd never forget. I think it's what kept me with him for way too long. He played terrible games with my head. For a month he'd be all over me, then completely ignore me until I'd be crying and wanting to die. It's like he turned on this piece of me and then decided to turn it off whenever he wanted to. I'd complain, but he'd say that as long as I was married, this is how it would have to be.

I would've left my husband until I caught this man with another woman. She came to me in the office to tell me, not knowing I had been with him. I got mad and went straight to him, and he explained it away by saying that we hadn't been involved for weeks, and again since I was unwilling to leave my husband yet, he'd have to keep his options open. I haven't been with him since, but he still opened something in me that I haven't been able to act on with my husband. He's still so distant and really only sees me as a mom to our kids. I don't think I'll ever cheat again. It made more trouble for me in the end.

Romance Is the Key to Meaningful Sex

Women in my study wanted much more romance in their lives. Satisfied women felt their husbands loved them and took the time and energy to show it in many ways, some of which we outlined in previous chapters. Women don't complain about having sex. They complain about having sex devoid of loving feeling and warmth. They don't want to have sex after they've been ignored, yelled at, humiliated, or unappreciated. Sex then becomes about the man just experiencing his own isolated pleasure, and that is an uncomfortable feeling for any woman.

Many men I've met are genuinely interested in pleasing their wives in the bedroom, but apparently for the majority of women, it isn't happening enough. Sex cannot be about intercourse. It has to be about an entire connection that develops with the focus on romance. Men and women have to put time and energy into making their sexual lifestyle one that is pleasurable for both of them. That begins with the romance that happens way before you are both naked. As one woman in my study put it, "The look in his eyes when I walked into the room . . ." Consider the many kind things each of you can do to show a loving interest in each other. Having great sex is not only about technique, although we will discuss that in detail. It really is about setting the mood, and that happens all day.

When was the last time you told your partner how beautiful or handsome she or he is? How often have you pointed out how sexy your partner is? And men have got to get it straight: women don't want to hear dirty remarks about their bodies. I have yet to hear a woman say, "I love it when I'm doing dishes and he comes up from behind and cops a feel or pinches my butt hard." I'm not sure what world these men are living in, but someone has to draw them a map about women. Women want to be wooed. No, they're not delicate flowers that don't want to participate in the pleasantries of sexual romance. They too want to say sexy things to their partners, and enjoy the flirting. But women want it to remain kind and lovely, not down and dirty.

Women say they try to get this message across, but I find that it's usually in the form of an angered response to something their husband has said or done. We all tend to be a little more reactive than proactive. It's better if a woman can approach her husband at a calm time and be clear about how it's in his interest to be romantic. Saying something like, "Honey, I want to have a lot more sex and I want to have more fun with it all. Can we talk about how we can do that?" should get his attention. Telling him that you want to join with him to make it special and frequent is a good message for either sex. Then discuss what each of you would like. That's the time for a woman to describe some of the romantic things she'd like him to do. As we've discussed, women sometimes have to spell out certain things in the beginning to help men get the specific ideas.

KRIS'S STORY

The Sex Was Good but It Was More about the Connection

My husband and I were married for eleven years when we moved out of state for me to take a job. We were happy together but once we moved, my husband didn't want to go back to work. I lost respect for him. We were financially drowning, and I was disappointed in my husband's failure in the business world. He wasn't supporting me financially or emotionally. I was the breadwinner and I didn't want to be. Our sex life suffered. He just avoided me and turned to pornography. I felt like he had left me emotionally.

I had one brief fling, and then one long affair. I met both men at work. The sex was good but it was more about the connection, especially with the longer affair. It made me feel alive and attractive. He took me to movies and we exercised together. I didn't want to end my marriage, but I couldn't get what I needed from my husband. My husband has since passed away, and I occasionally hear from the man I had the affair with. We would still be seeing each other if I hadn't moved back home. We both wanted to stay in our marriages, but needed someone to talk to and have a physical connection to without the complications of marriage.

I have asked men what they think their wives want in the area of romance. I have yet to find a husband who could not articulate many suggestions that his wife said she'd be happy with. So for many men, it's not that they don't have a clue, but that like everything else with marriage, who has the time? People get too swept away with life and lose focus—even on sex! When couples openly discuss their agreement to put more time and energy into sex, which translates to romance first, changes happen immediately.

So to begin putting romance back in your relationship, each of you can start by creating a list of what you think your partner would want in the area of romance. Review each other's list, placing stars next to your partner's best suggestions. Feel free to fill in any ideas that might be missing and return the list to your partner. Commit to doing the things on the list immediately; it will build the basis for a wonderfully meaningful sexual relationship for any couple. It may sound so simple, but most couples avoid being open about sex and then lament how disconnected they are sexually. The activity of making the lists itself will get the two of you focused and talking about making this part of your relationship great.

Through the experience of romance, men and women build sexual arousal and awareness. They send messages of love and desire, and this gives assurance that the man isn't just trying to satisfy himself. He is allowing himself to find his wife attractive as a whole being. He's complimenting and appreciating all parts of who she is. He's spending time with her and giving her attention because he wants to be with her and be connected to her. Romance says, "I want to be connected as a partner in this life process." He's no longer diminishing her by seeing her only as a sex object. He's valuing her beauty inside and out. Feeling valued builds tremendous trust within a woman and gives her the green light to allow herself to consider getting lost in their sexual relationship.

Differences between the Male and Female Orgasm: What Everyone Needs to Know

All of the trust and desire can still fall flat unless both partners are aware of some crucial information on how their physical bodies work sexually. Here's where it gets complicated. Men will have an orgasm through intercourse. The majority of women, however (anywhere from 50 to 75 percent) will not achieve orgasm through vaginal stimulation alone. In other words, intercourse will likely not cause a woman to achieve orgasm. Women do have strong sexual feelings from that stimulation; but to reach orgasm they need to have clitoral stimulation as well as, or even independent of, vaginal stimulation.

The clitoris has more nerve endings per area than anywhere else on the male or female body, and therefore is crucial to the female sexual experience. This little knob of skin located at the top of the vaginal opening can be stimulated, and an orgasm can be reached through that form of stimulation with or without intercourse. There are sexual positions that are purported to have the penis stimulating the clitoris during intercourse, but it would seem that one needs to be double-jointed to accomplish this feat. Surely, those positions don't allow for enough control to stimulate the clitoris in a way that is best for the woman.

Part of great sex for a woman is for her to have an awareness of how her own body works. There is no reason any man on earth should have a storehouse of knowledge about how to stimulate his partner's clitoris; after all, he doesn't own one himself. That's why it's best for a woman to masturbate (89 percent of women report that they have masturbated, so clearly it's normal) and allow herself to become familiar with the type of pressure and motion that works for her. It is never exactly the same for all women. Naturally, that pressure and motion might need to be changed during the sexual experience, and again, a man can't possibly read her mind. Most women do masturbate, but again, because society sends many mixed messages to women about their sexuality, many women are unwilling to let themselves go and really enjoy their bodies. Add a man to the mix and many women feel even more embarrassed to take control of their pleasure. Unfortunately, because sexual differences between men and women are complicated enough, a woman who is unwilling to explore her own sexuality is likely to make the mutual sexual experience more complicated. A woman is best served by getting to know her body, learning how to reach orgasm on her own through clitoral stimulation, and then bringing that knowledge to her sexual experience with her husband so that there is greater chance that she will reach orgasm with him.

Unfortunately, when a woman doesn't know her body and largely depends on her partner to make it all happen, there can be grave disappointment all around. He'll achieve orgasm through intercourse; and if she doesn't, there's a sense on his part that he can't please her, and a sense on her part that "He had fun, but what about me?" It doesn't leave the couple with a feeling of connectedness. Every sexual experience doesn't have to be a "wow," but it is a bad idea to leave a woman's sexuality in the hands of a man. When she has awareness of how to achieve orgasm, she can direct her partner on how to please her, or she can take matters into her own hand, literally.

A simple and highly useful technique is for the clitoris to be stimulated during intercourse by the woman herself. This allows her full awareness, and she will not need to give any directions. She can manage the pressure and motion and get herself to orgasm when she wants. It provides her with some greater measure of control over her body, which may also help her "let loose" emotionally, as we discussed before. There are sexual positions that better allow a woman to have her hand comfortably in the right spot, and a couple can explore those. Otherwise, the man can stimulate her clitoris with his hand before and during intercourse. This technique is also great, as it allows the woman free rein to enjoy the time without "working." But she will have to give some direction to her husband as to the pressure and motion.

Sex Facts

- The majority of women do *not* reach orgasm solely through vaginal stimulation (intercourse).
- Men usually do reach orgasm through intercourse.
- Women do reach orgasm through clitoral stimulation.
- The average woman takes twelve to twenty minutes to reach orgasm.
- The average man takes one to seven minutes to reach orgasm.

Noises like moans and groans can help tell him he's on the right track, but it likely won't be enough. She will have to use words: "softer," "harder," "stay right there" . . . and if she is uncomfortable doing so she'll likely get frustrated, which upsets the entire process. Then he feels frustrated, and suddenly a wonderful time turns into a complete failure.

Men and Sexual Technique

Men have to learn that they do not have advanced degrees in sexuality either. Some men have the idea that they have to be able to do it all for their woman, which is archaic. They think that if they were good lovers, their wives would love intercourse and would orgasm just like that. Trust me and science, I don't care if you're Don Juan and Casanova combined, science beats your inflated ego every time. A man who feels that it is all up to him to please his wife sexually may see her own stimulation of her clitoris, or her using an object such as a vibrator to help her achieve orgasm, as an affront to his ability. His reasoning is simple. Without her stimulation she wouldn't have an orgasm, and therefore, he proves to himself that he cannot please her on his own. This is true, but let's get to the other part of the truth.

A man's ability to please his wife sexually is only about his ability to make her feel loved, desired, and safe. That is what allows her to truly enjoy herself, let herself go, and want to have an orgasm with her husband. His pleasing her is not going to have to do solely with the size of his penis, but rather the size of his heart. The warmth and appreciation he offers are what will cause his wife to give herself permission to become lost in him and have really great sex. Men need to stop worrying about how good they are in bed and be really concerned with how good they are out of bed.

Toward this end, the sex also needs to be about a couple's love for each other. Many women said that the man they cheated with told them how beautiful and wonderful they were during foreplay and intercourse; something their husbands never did. In order for sex to be about connection, there needs to be a sense of love tied up within it. That allows for greater trust from a woman. Again, every sexual experience with a spouse is not going to be all that, but almost all of them can have an obvious element of love, with some very simple loving comments and a focus on each other's pleasure. Yes, women can be comfortable with or even aroused by different forms of sexual play. Science is still studying that. But surely for any woman, getting in touch with her deeper arousal and her willingness to explore and try new things is going to be tied up in how much she trusts her mate.

As a man comes to understand that his wife's ability to reach orgasm or not with intercourse alone in no way relates to his own sexual abilities, the woman will become more comfortable exploring methods that work for her. One common practice is the use of a vibrator. There are many different types of vibrators, so a woman needs to find the kind best suited to her and her partner. Some are labeled as "personal massagers" and sold at regular stores like Brookstone, for those who feel uncomfortable shopping in a sex shop. They can be small, about the size of a pen. A smaller vibrator allows for simpler use during intercourse. Instead of either partner using a hand, the vibrator can be held on the clitoris by either person as a method for getting a woman to reach orgasm during intercourse. Men have to become comfortable with the idea of a vibrator if women choose to use one—again, it shows their willingness to be totally open to sexual play and pleasure. They have begun to feel a sense of comfort and trust, allowing them to enjoy being with their partners in that way. Women are entitled to enjoy feeling sexual, and it's better to invite it all into the joined sexual experience.

SUSAN'S STORY
What Happened When He Found My Vibrator

My husband was so angry when he saw my vibrator. He thought I was cheating because of it, I don't know why. I explained to him that my therapist had suggested it and he was very angry at her. I agreed to stop using it, but my therapist convinced me to talk to him about it. He suffers from low self-esteem, so I think this really crushed him. He knows that I have a much stronger libido than he does, and I'm pretty sure that the vibrator really just added insult to injury.

My therapist suggested that she talk to both of us just about this, and I couldn't believe it when he agreed. He later told me that he was scared if he didn't, I'd cheat on him. I felt so bad he'd worry about that. I would never do that. My therapist was really great at helping him understand not to take it all personally. It still disturbed my husband that I would masturbate and have an orgasm without him involved. But he didn't want to have sex often enough, so my therapist convinced us to have him be involved with my own pleasure. I was more than happy to do this, and it has been great. It has really led us to have a lot more sex. Just going to the therapist seemed to open his eyes that people could change or something, so he went on his own and got on an antidepressant and is considering Viagra. Things are much better and we've really gotten along overall much better.

Closer to Orgasm

Beyond understanding how orgasms work for men and women, it is equally important to understand that timing is everything. The average woman takes anywhere from twelve to twenty minutes to reach orgasm, while the average man takes anywhere from one minute to just over seven minutes with steady vaginal thrusting. For most men it'll take longer to achieve orgasm if they're having sex more frequently, but usually it will still take his partner longer to get there. So what often happens is that a wife will stimulate her husband either manually or orally and then immediately after, they'll have intercourse. Because the man has already been somewhat stimulated, his likelihood of having an orgasm quickly during intercourse is greater. Too often, even with any kind of clitoral stimulation, there is just no way she'll reach orgasm anywhere close to him unless he slows his pace and stops thrusting to prevent his orgasm.

This discrepancy has caused great frustration and dissatisfaction in couples' lives. Men often rush to the intercourse part, so the clock is ticking. If the woman is not close to an orgasm, there is an excellent chance that the man will reach orgasm before her. Soon after his orgasm, his penis will likely become flaccid while her mind comes around to the frustrating fact that he's done and she's not even close. Either partner could continue to stimulate her clitoris, but after either a male or female has an orgasm, the impetus to please the other quickly diminishes. In fact, science has shown that for men, there is a physical process that makes him sleepy right after orgasm. In other words, after sex is not at all the best time for him to focus on managing his partner's orgasm.

In my years of counseling couples, I've learned a great way to overcome this obstacle: the man should focus on getting the woman closer to orgasm while he takes a break. While a man is sexually excited, he's typically willing to be extremely attentive to his partner. For a man, actions that please his partner are often turn-ons for himself, so the best time for him to put energy into helping his partner achieve or get very close to orgasm is when he is already aroused. Here's one simple yet very effective method: first, the woman spends time arousing the man. (He can also arouse her at the same time, if the couple prefers.) Next, she stops arousing him, and he focuses on arousing her. Once she is much closer to an orgasm, he can enter her and continue to stimulate her clitoris. Intercourse will begin with her already on her way to having an orgasm and he will have had a break, allowing him to last longer before having an orgasm. At the same time, she'll have a much better chance of having enough time to have an orgasm during intercourse. She will still have to find a way to express how close she is to an orgasm, so he can slow down or speed up his thrusting to control his response. Don't pass up this opportunity to make sex great. Just discussing it will bring the two of you closer because you'll open communication about your sex life.

For his part, a man needs to understand that foreplay doesn't only involve pleasing a woman sexually, it also includes saying loving things to her, giving hugs and soft kisses, giving her a regular massage in which he feels her body more, telling her how much he loves her . . . whatever she'd like him to add to the experience to make it even better for her. Some men missed that day in school and nobody told them these things are necessary. They may need coaching—not in some distant "I can't believe I have to draw him a map" way, but rather in a passionate "I trust that he wants to journey with me and let me let loose with him" sort of way. The more they get this coaching, the more the men will learn to make this type of loving foreplay a part of the sexual experience on a regular basis.

The G-spot

There has been debate over this elusive spot located inside the vagina. Many in the medical establishment were unsure if it really existed. Recently, doctors have used MRI scans and biopsies to prove that the G-spot does exist. It is located about an inch or two up from the vaginal opening. It is highly sensitive tissue that triggers intense sexual satisfaction when touched the right way. There's much to learn about finding it for yourselves as a couple, as well as sexual positions that will likely stimulate this internal spot. It's worth exploring and learning all about it together.

Having an orgasm around the same time can be very meaning-ful and help a couple avoid frustration, but some couples have rea-sons that it doesn't work. She takes a really long time. He has difficulty waiting that long even if he earnestly tries. Every couple

Tips for Better Sex

- Talk at a calm time about how to make sex more satisfy-ing and frequent for both of you.

- The man needs to understand a woman's connection between romance, trust, and great sex.

- Turn up the music or TV to drown out any sexual sounds.

- Lock your door.

- The woman's clitoris should be stimulated before and during intercourse.

- The woman should be minutes away from orgasm as intercourse starts.

- The man should use erotic massage, say loving things, give compliments during sex.

- The woman should verbally tell a man what is working or not working for her during sex.

- Both partners should avoid jokes that poke fun at each other's sexual behavior.

- Couples can explore interesting ideas, try things as long as they are not painful or embarrassing to either person.

has to discover how things work best for them. For example, if he has difficulty having or maintaining an erection due to medications he's taking, she's not going to stop stimulating him if it'll mean he'll lose his erection and have to take a long time to deal with that. In such a case they'll move straight to intercourse and she may not have time to get herself to orgasm. Whatever the case, they can be creative and figure it out. In this example, she can have an orgasm before he has his erection. He can focus on her clitoris whether orally or manually, and he can tell her wonderfully romantic things, and she can have a wonderfully connected experience with her partner even though she didn't have an orgasm during intercourse. Then, the couple can switch their attention to pleasing him. Or they can switch the order. It doesn't matter. It only matters that the sex be about the love and desire, the message that each of you greatly desires the other and loves the whole of your partner. The message that you both want to let go and be intertwined and connected in this way is what will fuel great sex far more than anything else.

Touch Matters More than You Think

Many women wrote in describing how important touch was for them. Unfortunately, they often were describing how much better the man they cheated with was at touching them than their husbands were.

In the 1950s Harry Harlow conducted a well-known study of newborn monkeys that revealed a powerful message about touch. Newborn monkeys were given two artificially constructed surrogate mothers. One model was made of wire and contained a steady supply of milk; the other was also made of wire but because it was wrapped in terry cloth, it was warm but lacked any source of nourishment. The infant monkeys tended to spend time with the soft yet foodless mother, even coming close to starvation as a result of their preference.

The study proved the importance of warm touch from mother to child. It also told us something about each and every one of us: we yearn to touch and be touched. Men and women want to feel loved through touch, and a quick loving touch is often the simplest, quickest, and most effective way to connect and provide a loving moment. Start touching each other more, stand closer together, take the opportunity to cuddle instead of sitting apart, be freer with kisses and hugs. Create an environment where the focus to love never leaves and is easily supported with simple loving physical gestures. As a couple, decide to count for three days in a row how many times each of you lovingly touch the other and are touched. If it's not enough, the solution is simple.

You have a statistically greater possibility of having sex more often if you touch each other more. It makes sense that the more we physically touch each other, the more comfortable we become with physical intimacy.

Finding the Time for Sex

There's no doubt that the greatest nemesis to great, frequent sex is time. Who has the time to sit around and focus on sex? By the time bedtime rolls around and every chore has been accomplished, most people are plain exhausted, so they do not readily desire sex or have anything more than just a "Get it over with" attitude. Some women say that they feel like they have another job dealing with the sex thing. But for the vast majority of women who are dissatisfied with sex, they want sex to be better and to have it more often.

It's funny that sex can lead to children, and children are often the source of an interrupted sexual lifestyle. When the kids are possibly lurking in the hall, or worse yet can enter your bedroom freely, that'll take the fun and romance out of sex in a heartbeat. Couples who don't think about how to make the time for sex and make it great tend not to have much sex at all. Perhaps couples are waiting for some Hollywoodesque moment of passion to overwhelm them so that spontaneously they'll be ripping their clothes off and doing it on the kitchen table—oh yeah, but what about the child who wants more macaroni and cheese, oops.

Part of making love is talking together about not only how to make it great once you're together in the throes of passion, but how to carve out the time and space to have it in the first place. Again, this is not an individual maneuver. It seems that women typically have the ultimate responsibility to get kids bathed and in bed with their homework done, whether or not they work outside the home. Too many women say they're exhausted and just not feeling it when their husbands bounce into bed ready for sex. Couples have to work together. Women can again let their partners know how much they also want to have sex, and suggest that tiredness is one stumbling block. This way, the couple can commit to cleaning up together, getting the kids to bed together, or the man can surely decide to take over some of these activities. Yes, there are men who do this already, but I dare say most of the time, couples do not communicate about how to find the energy for sex.

Furthermore, sex is always going to be different when there are others around. No couple wants to hear a knock on the door right after sex from an adolescent asking if everything is okay because he heard some strange noises. Or have their six-year old ask if there was a cat in the room because she heard cat noises last night, as one woman related during my study. Seclude yourselves and turn on music or the television loud enough that you're sure it'll drown out any noises. You still might not feel completely comfortable to let loose, but it'll be a great step in the right direction.

Rid Yourself of Sexual Obstacles

Here's another consideration while you're wondering how you can have more frequent, satisfying sex. Many couples live a lifestyle that allows for regular sighting of their spouse using the bathroom facilities. Please consider avoiding this. All of us understand the reality of life and time management, two people sharing a bathroom, rushed and hurried. But over the long haul observing our spouse in less than appealing situations can take a toll. Keep in mind that reality will dictate that we will already have to see our spouse in compromising positions. There will be illness and procedures and plenty of physical ailments that will more than fill our cups of the real world. But those tend to be inconsistent and chalked up to necessity. When you regularly view your partner on the toilet, it can add up to a vision that directly or indirectly diminishes your sexual attraction. I'm all for realness between couples, and do not suggest people should hide ailments or weaknesses. But you are entitled to request that there be private bathroom time (with a little respectful time-management cooperation).

Don't Make Your Partner Feel Self-Conscious

I've had husbands and wives complain that their partner doesn't come prepared for sex with a cleanliness quotient that works for both of them. There is nothing wrong with asking for or being asked to clean up before sex. Another issue is certain jokes commonly made by men that cause women to feel self-conscious. Sex lends itself to fun and play, so it's not unusual to have some joking. But men should be cautious not to make any joke that pokes fun at a characteristic or action of their wives, verbal or otherwise. Surely men can understand this, because they typically don't want their wives making fun of something that goes wrong with them during sex or anything that would make them feel less than sexually capable. When partners do this, they make the other person feel embarrassed, and that leads to immediate inhibition and sadly, less trust to let go and just enjoy being together.

Dealing with Molestation Issues

Sadly, when I asked women the question "Was anyone ever sexually inappropriate toward you at any point from birth until age twenty?" a terribly high number was reported by both groups: 43 percent from the cheating group and 38 percent from the faithful group. Clearly, because there is only a 5 percent difference, this statistic proves that sexual inappropriateness does not on average have a direct effect on the fidelity of a woman. But it does tell us all that we as a society have a great deal of work to do to reduce and obliterate this number. It is for a later time and book of my own to help in this much-needed area, but for the purpose of what we're discussing here, there is too great a chance that a woman in a relationship has suffered from her past. Even though it might not correlate to cheating, it still can greatly affect the sexuality of a woman.

For every woman who is aware that she has been molested (some block it out or know it happened but choose to not focus on it or tell anyone) it's better to recognize it and discuss it with her husband whom she trusts. Sexuality can be even more complicated when issues of control, dominance, and shame are left over from the past. Men need to become fully aware of how important it is to stay away from sexual play that may tap into memories of molestation of the past. That is why men need to ask directly what works and what doesn't work for their partners. Often, this group of women may choose to use a position that puts them in greater control until they get to a point of complete trust in the sexual relationship. Again, this is not the place to elaborate in detail on how couples can overcome past tragedies such as this, but at the very least, bringing it into the open with tremendous sensitivity and respect for the woman's issues is the best solution.

There are also those women who weren't molested but who received very negative or shameful messages about sex. It's important for men to be aware that those messages exist and to discuss them in an open and caring manner so that they can be put to rest. One woman told me she is still haunted by her first kissing encounter with a boyfriend. She was enjoying the feeling of connection and attractiveness when his mother came in and said, "There'll be none of that. What kind of girl are you?" and then fixed her with a shaming look. She was made to feel embarrassed, and sometimes that shame came up and interfered with her ability to let go and enjoy. This woman deserves to put this memory to rest, to hear that there will be much of *that*: much love, pleasure, enjoyment, and sexual fulfillment. So there! If you are able to listen to your partner talk about early experiences with supportive love, you will allow the sexual relationship to reach greater levels, and you will unblock a great deal of energy, making way for greater pleasure and connection.

TRACY'S STORY
My Cheating Is Connected to My Childhood

I cannot say for certain that my childhood experiences with sex, my relationship with my parents, and their relationship with each other affected my behavior, but I think it is reasonable to assume that they did. I don't know what it is like to be raised in a "normal" emotionally healthy family; therefore, I don't know if my actions would have been different if I had been. I do have one very good friend who was raised in an extremely normal, wonderful family, and she is about as wonderful a wife and mother as you could possibly find. She is also the one friend I would never tell that I had an affair. I wish I could take it all back.

I wish that I could forget it and let it go. No amount of prayer can make the guilt go away. I try to rationalize with myself that those men had just as much to do with what happened as I did, but I never get very far. The truth is that it just wouldn't have happened had I not allowed it to.

I think after the first time I had an affair I was angry with myself, but I was also angry at my husband (fiancé at the time) that he could forgive me for it, because I would not have done so if I were in his shoes. Then it happened again, and I wanted him to leave me. I mean, what kind of person stays with a person who does that to you? I wanted him to leave me to prove to me that I was not worth it, that I was too much trouble. But he's still here. And I am thankful for that now.

My dad (who actually is my stepdad) and my mother were married when I was six and divorced when I was seventeen. Before they were married, my mother had an affair with an old friend of hers. Then when I was about sixteen, my mother began an affair with a man from work. One day he showed up at our house with my mom to get all the furniture. I was not allowed to go with them and she left me behind with my stepdad. My stepdad had been taking advantage of me sexually for years, so much so that I actually thought of him more as a lover when I was a teenager. When my mom cheated on him and wanted to divorce him, I thought he'd take me away and make me his wife. When he left, I felt so rejected. I feel sick and ashamed just writing it. I had been raped when I was fifteen, and no one said anything about it except for my stepdad, who told me that's what I get for hanging around with that race of people. After the rape was when my stepdad started having sex with me.

My mother had suspected that my stepdad was having an affair, and I almost died because I felt like maybe he was cheating on me too. I finally moved out when I was seventeen and moved in with my brother. Today, I no longer have any relationship with my stepdad, but I don't know who my real dad is because my mother won't tell me. Despite all this, my relationship with my mother has really improved dramatically over the years. She is a pretty good grandmother to my children. There came a day when I decided that I did not want to repeat my mother's life. I want to have a successful, happy marriage and a fantastic relationship with my children. It would be great, though, if I could go back and undo all the bad.

If you find yourself wondering and struggling with molestation from the past, do yourself a favor and be self-deserving enough to talk to someone in your area who's an expert in this field, or seek out support groups through the local hospitals. Don't allow the bad people of your life to continue to molest you and rob you of the good life moments that you deserve and will have to take back for yourself. Be kind to yourself.

Choose Birth Control That Puts Your Mind at Ease

Many women have shared with me that their concerns about becoming pregnant weigh on their sexually active minds. If a couple doesn't want to get pregnant, it's a good idea to deal with birth control. It makes for better sex. Maybe both of you don't think it's on your mind, but unless you are confident in your birth control methods, one or both of you will subtly direct yourselves away from good, frequent sex. There could be concern about positions, ovulation times, or frequency leading to greater odds of pregnancy. Be sure that if either of you is unsure of the birth control methods being used, sex is a latent enemy. Figure this one out, whether through thorough education and conversations with a physician or clear talk with your partner about who's doing what to provide reliable birth control.

JACKIE'S STORY
I Would Have Cheated

I was about to cheat. My husband found an e-mail and it wasn't completely out there but it was suggestive. I just blew it off, but we both knew things were not going well. We sat down and talked about sex. It was so strange because we *never* talked about sex. We'd been married eight years and had two babies so we had stopped having sex a long time ago. I really thought it was me, that I was turned off or maybe when I had my last baby something physical happened that just turned off my sex drive.

But I knew that wasn't it when I met the guy I started flirting with. I hadn't been that excited since college. It was just the way he touched me, gently, like he was devouring me. We played a game through e-mail and some dirty talk, a little phone sex. But when my husband caught me with this e-mail, I froze and came back to reality. What was I doing? Two kids and a marriage to a decent guy, even if we never had sex, or just now and then.

When we spoke I learned that he had actually gone so far

as to kiss a girl on a trip a few months back, and he said he stopped it there. I'm not sure I believe him, but I don't think I could judge him because I was going there too. We were pretty depressed about it and we spent a few days thinking about whether to divorce or not. But both of us really wanted to keep our family together and were still kind of interested in each other. It's so crazy how you can just turn off to your husband because the two of you just become different people, mom and dad. I became a teacher and he was an architect. When we were faced with leaving each other, we didn't really feel so into each other, but I think we started off by making a logical decision. Why not try to make the marriage work? We had so much to gain.

We planned a trip away for the first time in years without any kids. It was unbelievable. Neither of us could imagine that we'd be able to slip back into having fun sex so quickly like when we were first married. It really was like riding a bicycle. We got some books and a video on making sex better and it really changed things. I still worry about how close we got to throwing it all away and wonder whether that could happen again. But for now we're still having sex, probably not nearly as much as both of us would want, but enough to make us satisfied and not go looking around.

Try Anything Safe

Now that we know that both men and women want satisfying and regular sex, you can explore that with your partner. No more myths about women not wanting much or better sex. Yes, there are significant gender differences in sexuality, but desire for having it and enjoying it is not one of them. Sexuality is really about being in love and making love. That is something that extends to every part of your couplehood. Don't wait to have sex in your bedroom late at night. Extend the romance and love of sexuality to all parts of your day with little touches, phone calls, thoughtful presents, and gestures that will all serve to connect the two of you throughout your day. Then you'll be using sexuality as a beautiful way to lose yourselves in each other and connect in a way you haven't connected before.

When you have a trusting sexual relationship, you can try anything. Many couples are searching for interesting new forms of sexual play so as to keep their sex lives from being run-of-the-mill. I find that sometimes these couples do not have good sex lives; they lack the romance, trust, and warmth, and they have a lot to learn in general about the physiology of men and women. Sometimes, one or both partners are seeking to enhance their sexuality by skipping over healthier techniques out of ignorance or other issues. If you are not satisfied sexually, or not happy with how often you're having sex, the answer isn't unusual sex toys or unusual sex games. That may help you have a little more sex and maybe enjoy it more, but it's not going to deal with the problem that the two of you are not allowing yourselves to be connected sexually. It also could take your sex life to an uncomfortable place, because in order for both of you to try something very different and enjoy it, you need to start with a trusting, loving relationship. Otherwise, you risk embarrassment or resentment from the partner who agreed to try something unusual at the other partner's suggestion and was hurt when it turned into a bad experience. You should both broach the real issues in your sex life, which as explained have to do with your whole relationship.

However, if you have a satisfying sex life or are on your way to dealing with relationship issues and want to try new sexual things, there is nothing wrong with new ideas. No person should feel uncomfortable trying something new one time, as you are with someone you greatly trust and are comfortable being vulnerable with. That person would never want to have a partner do something that would be painful or humiliating. And that's the rule of thumb. If trying something new is painful, humiliating, embarrassing, or illegal, either partner can decline with that explanation. There are so many sexual activities that do not include these issues that partners are able to figure out new things to do without bumping into any of these. If your partner is insistent, it's time to talk to a friend or visit a therapist to determine whether what's being asked of you is commonly considered taboo or if perhaps you own the problem by seeing a normal and healthy request as humiliating.

All in all, the privacy involved in discussing and trying new sexual play is very connecting to a couple, as it allows them to share in more and different pleasure reserved only for the two of them. Make sure to always keep your private lives just that. Keep building your trust and connection through your romance and sexuality.

PART TWO

Connecting to Love

7

Turn Back Time, Just Have Fun

Among faithful women, 68 percent reported that they wanted to go out with their husbands more frequently. It's uncanny that what causes us to fall in love and decide to get married is the very thing we tend to stay far away from once we are married. We dated, had fun, took the time to talk politics and philosophy, and giggled along the way. But now? Couples barely know the lighter side of each other, and there comes a point too often when they don't even know what to do to have fun together anymore. Enjoying your partner is not like having your cabinet stocked with chocolate. It is not always going to be there to enjoy whenever you decide to get back to it.

Dating is often a great part of our overall courtship with our partners, so why not backtrack and remember why you fell in love in the first place? It's a simple investment that pays immediate dividends. Plan to spend a minimum of two hours per week and do something entertaining. Turn back time and remember what it was like to be young again (even if you met each other when you were older). Bring youth back into your lives and use that energy to build the lightness and fun back into your lives. Ideally, turn back time the same night every week so that both of you know never to make other plans unless something crucial arises that must take precedence (in which case you'd plan for a different night to go out).

Turning back time means getting yourselves in the mood for being young. Play the music from your youth, visit the same or similar places you'd go to when you dated, have some interesting topics ready for discussion, as hopefully you did when you were courting. For the first Turn Back Time night, role play—pretend that you are on your first date, and spend the whole evening learning about each other. Put some effort in. Remember happy times, be especially courteous. Even just going out and having coffee or taking a walk, with the right attitude, can be special. Pick up a small, inexpensive gift for each other. Ask each other questions and really listen to the responses.

Make it a time that is just for the two of you, not with another couple. Let's face it, when couples go out together, the men and women tend to split up and go off in conversation with each other. It can be great fun, but is not time when spouses grow together as a private couple. You can ask friends to meet you after your two hours on that night if you'd like.

Each of you can take turns planning Turn Back Time night. You don't want to end up getting into the car and looking curiously at each other, wondering what to do now—never a positive

Turn Back Time Night

- Choose the same evening each week to go out alone for a minimum of two hours.
- Play music from your youth.
- Do the same things, or visit the same kinds of places, that you used to when you dated.
- Review the newspaper for local happenings—consider aloud what you both can do to have fun.
- Each of you takes turns planning the night.
- Do not talk about three things: work, money, or kids.

moment. It says that neither of you has taken enough care to plan anything. Find interesting things to do—they'll provide a backdrop to better discussions and more fun times together.

Every couple needs some private space to develop a personality that is free of life's stressors. Remember when you had a song that was just for the two of you? Was the title something like, "Kids and Mortgage Payments and My Damn Boss?" I don't think so. It was about love. Focus on two people seeing something wonderful in each other that no one else took the time to see. Take the time to notice it and get back to being a unit with your own personality, inside jokes, and secrets. Find a new song already. Be young and in love for at least two hours a week on your date night. Soon you'll be singing a new song and feeling younger, even when you're not on a date. Do it for your relationship and as a life enhancer. Be romantic.

Creating Private Space for Your Relationship

Limit your children's access to your bedroom. There are many other rooms in your home. I'm not suggesting that there be some fanatical restrictions, but just a healthy respect for your space. Your children need to learn that this is their parents' room and it is only to be entered when permission is given.

Lock your bedroom door. When the children are settled, sequester yourselves by closing and locking the door. It doesn't imply that you're locking your children out. It only says that you and your spouse want and deserve some private uninterrupted time. If your children need access in the middle of the night, a simple tap can work.

Give yourself permission to find time with your partner. Even if time with your spouse occasionally comes at the expense of your children, remember how crucial it is for your children to have parents who are in love.

Keep work out of the bed. Once you're alone in your bedroom, don't invite other intense pieces of life into it.

Make the bedroom a haven. We typically spend money or time on the rooms in our homes where people visit. We should have the same commitment to making the bedroom inviting for us.

SALLY'S STORY
Nothing in Common Except the Kids

The first time I cheated, it was with my husband's best friend. It was shameful, and that's not the worst of it. The only reason it stopped was because the best friend had to move out of town to deal with a family issue. I've cheated since then, but it hasn't been about a real relationship; I'm just trying to add some fun to my life. I've been married seventeen years, have four kids, and can't remember the last time my husband and I had fun alone, completely alone. I really think that he's cheated on me. No, I know he has. All the signs have been there, but I can't ask him about it because I'm afraid he'll turn the same questions on me, and I'm not willing to go there.

The sick thing is that the man I cheated with is a playboy, and I knew it was never going to lead to any real long-term relationship. I'd never leave my husband for him. He couldn't begin to provide the consistency or maturity of life that I and my kids would need. But we had the best times together. We'd laugh so much. I've never laughed that much with my husband. We'd meet out late when my husband thought I was with my girlfriend going to the movies or listening to some music. She covered for me, but I hated the fact that my husband would much rather I go have fun with my best girlfriend than be with him. It was like a burden was lifted for him, although I'm now pretty sure it gave him the time to do what he wanted. He always has something to do at work. I think we just both have closed our eyes for a while.

My husband and I don't have anything in common after seventeen years, except our four wonderful children. I feel terrible that my children have been raised thinking that their parents' marriage is normal. How sick is that?

JUDITH'S STORY
Kids Came First, Second, and Third

I thought my husband would leave when he found out about my cheating. He was so hurt when he discovered us, it was horrible. I wished he'd be angry instead, but the look on his face was just so pained. I'll never forget and I'll never cheat again, if only to never hurt him like that again. I didn't really cheat on *him.* I now say I cheated on life. It didn't have much to do with him, as much as that I was feeling so old and worn. I was all about the children. They were going to have the best school projects, the best home where all their friends would come, the best of everything. I researched their activities and spent so much time shuttling them back and forth, I was constantly involved, cooked, cleaned, you know. . . . I didn't think I was doing anything wrong. In fact, I was mad at my husband that I was working so hard and he was putting demands on me. After all, he's an adult. He shouldn't be trying to take my time away from the kids to have sex and go away with him.

By the time I came up for air, we had built completely different lives. I was into yoga and exercise, he was into country music and chili. He was enjoying the great chili cook-off and I was working out like a fiend. Frankly, I wanted to change my body and he refused to pay for plastic surgery, so I was going to show him. The irony was that he never complained about my body. That was all me. I cheated with the trainer not because I loved him or anything, but I was looking to reaffirm myself after being a mom. I wanted to show myself I was still hot and could make heads turn.

My husband is a simple, kind guy who just wanted some of my attention. He's not a saint; he admits he could drink much less. But he only wanted to spend more time with me for those years, and I just wouldn't do it. After a while, he stopped asking, and I thought that meant we were finally okay with our signals and that we were doing just fine. When I started cheating, I just didn't care. I wasn't thinking. But when my husband caught me, I was devastated. It was like everything kicked in. What had I done? What was I about to do to my kids, after all the years I did everything for them, to completely screw it up with somebody I didn't even care about? My husband and I decided we did still love each other even though neither of us was "in love."

The first thing we did was hang out with each other more. My husband only agreed to stay with me if we really tried to be a couple again and spend time doing stuff. He began to exercise with me, which he badly needed to get his body in better shape and in better health. I started going with him to his country events, concerts, and get-togethers, and we started having a blast. I couldn't believe how quickly we found our old selves together again. It was like we were back in our twenties. It is so amazing how far we went from each other and how being in love was right there in front of us all along. I was just convinced that he was the problem instead of the solution. Sure, it's not perfect, but we are way out of the woods and my cheating is as if it happened to another person in another lifetime. You hear so many different things about marriage and can't imagine the bad things that happen to you. But you kick yourself when you see how it can come up in your own life.

. . .

No matter how far away from each other you've emotionally been, most couples can recapture their relationship with some solid commitment to renewing their loving spirit. Don't wait for your relationship to get that far away. Remember what brought you together and rediscover it regularly.

8

The Two-Week Connect
to Love Program

As we discussed in the introduction to this book, couples can overcome their struggles in a short period of time. There is one prerequisite, however, to quick success with this program: there must be two willing participants. The two of you must go through this program together as partners, not with one dragging an unwilling partner along for the ride. I have said before that the energy and efforts of only one partner can change a relationship, and of course that is true. But for a couple to reconnect *quickly*, much more of a team effort is required. If you're on your own here, following the other suggestions in the book will make a huge difference in your relationship. However, this program will likely fall short if only one partner follows it.

If you and your partner are looking to be more in love, add some romance, stop fighting as much, or give yourselves a chance to focus on each other, this reconnection program will start you in the right direction and likely make a dramatic difference. It is based on my twenty-three years of experience counseling couples combined with my research studies on both men and women in all parts of the world. For two people intent on finding love, great things can happen when you know where to put your energy.

The program is not meant to be a substitute for marital counseling. It is also not intended to deal with a prolonged history of pain, abuse, or cheating. My Reconnect to Love Day, which I mentioned in the introduction, can help couples who may be at the brink of divorce, but that program includes a unique analysis and understanding of the couple that I could not begin to offer in this written form. However, if you review this program and it looks good to you, it'll likely do a great deal to help you and your partner. If you review it and can't imagine jumping into the emotional and physical intimacy that's suggested, then it's not for you, and seeking professional help is the best idea.

Week One

Thursday Night

Plan the week ahead (Time commitment: Thirty minutes). Review the reconnection plan and your one-week calendar together and agree to follow through on all of the steps. It is worth postponing the program for a week or two in order to start on a week when you have the freedom to keep the one-week schedule.

When spending any time together as part of this program, it should be in a place that is comfortable, at a time when there will be no interruption, and when cell phones and such can be put away or turned off. None of the time used for this reconnection plan is to be spent watching television. You can watch television together after you complete the planned task for that day if you like.

Friday Night

Appreciate each other (Time commitment: One hour). Start out with a five-minute exercise: each of you should take the time to write five things that you appreciate about the other. No more than one item on the list should relate to your partner's external beauty. Each thing should be:

1. Specific
2. Personal
3. Recent

For example, instead of "You're so kind," write, "You made it a point to ask me how my day went on Wednesday and offered to make me tea." Instead of "You're such a great parent," write, "You make sure to hug the kids every day and tell them how special they are." Instead of "You are so beautiful/handsome," write, "I like your lovely smile and shining eyes." Instead of "You work so hard for us," write, "You had to deal with that miserable matter at work recently, and I know you work so hard for our benefit."

Remember that appreciation is not only about what someone does above and beyond the call of duty. We deserve to be appreciated and recognized even for efforts that we are supposed to make.

Facing each other, looking into each other's eyes, and holding hands, take turns saying each appreciative item on the list. Then embrace each other.

Spend the rest of the time discussing the events of the day, being sure to ask follow-up questions of your partner. This shows interest and willingness to learn more about your partner's feelings. As you listen, begin to imagine how your partner felt during the situation that is being recounted or how your partner feels presently during the discussion. You don't yet need to tell your partner what you think that feeling is, but begin to focus on it during this conversation and all subsequent ones. You can also choose to read next to each other while sharing some interesting points about what you are reading.

Do not have sex tonight.

Saturday

1. **Make breakfast together** (Time commitment: Forty-five minutes). Cook something together—pancakes, bagels, sausage, whatever you like, but you must do it as partners. If you have children, include them also. Prepare each other's plate and serve the food to each other. Talk to each other (and the kids) over the breakfast table. Spend the day as you wish, preferably on some outing together, though that's not necessary.

2. **Learn to listen and understand each other** (Time commitment: One hour). Set aside an hour to spend together at any point during the day. During this hour each of you takes a turn bringing up some issue that does not involve a criticism of your partner. For example, you can bring up how upset you are with your boss, sibling, child . . . but not how upset you are with your partner. Each of you must talk

about one negative issue or struggle you are dealing with. The listener:

- Asks follow-up questions, such as "What did you say to your sister when she said that?"
- Sums up what has been heard every few sentences in order to send the message that the listener is following the story clearly: "So she called to tell you that you should be sending her money for the party she wants to throw for your parents that you can't even make because she never asked you about it in the first place?"
- Shares how he/she thinks the talker must be feeling: "Unbelievable. You must've been kind of angry."

The talker gives the listener the opportunity to recap and gently corrects the listener when necessary.

Then, each partner takes a turn bringing up a positive issue to share. It should be something that does not involve the other person directly. The listener responds the same way.

"How did our kid look when she heard the teacher call out her name for the award?"

"She didn't even know she was getting the award and she was so excited."

"Wow, how exciting. I bet you were beaming."

The purpose of this exercise is to get the two of you into the habit of understanding each other. Obviously, it may feel very stilted, but you can never get to the real understanding you need in a relationship without the practice. Try to fill the time going back and forth discussing issues. If you still have time left, just chat about your past week and things you've been thinking about or news events or things you've read that have caught your interest.

Saturday Night

Build sexual desire (Time commitment: Thirty minutes). There will be no sex tonight. Undress each other and slowly embrace and/or dance for a couple of minutes. Lie down and take turns slowly stroking each other on all parts of the body except the genitals. While stroking your partner, say five loving things. Consider: "I love you so much," "You're the most wonderful person in my life," "Thanks for being you." As part of those five loving things, make a few positive comments about how attractive you find your partner and why.

Sunday

1. **Make breakfast together again** (Time commitment: Forty-five minutes).

2. **Turn Back Time night** (Time commitment: Two hours). The husband plans for a date either before or after eating dinner at home. The two of you can make dinner together or order takeout, but do not eat dinner out. The date must not involve a movie. Look in the weekend newspaper or online for entertaining events that you think both of you would like. Do not ask your wife what she wants to do. Plan something you think she'd like or surely know she wouldn't hate. (For example, don't buy tickets to a ball game if she has never watched a game in her life.) Consider a museum (for this option you may have to go out in the afternoon instead of the evening), a lounge with music, a concert, a bicycle ride if weather and health permit, or any other outing that sounds fun. On Turn Back Time night you should focus on getting back to youthfulness and not discussing any stressful subjects (work, money, or kids).

Sunday Night

Make love (Time commitment: One hour). For obvious reasons, you should have your favorite music playing in your room so that there are no distractions and you are not concerned with your children hearing you. You should also bring music, candles, incense, and whatever else makes the setting pleasant for both of you.

Listen and lead. This first lovemaking of this reconnection may be different for you. You are taking the time to understand and enjoy each other.

Begin by undressing each other. Then she lies down on the bed and he caresses her all over her body (except the genitals) for five minutes, saying loving things to her as he did the night before. She leads him by telling him what she'd like him to do to bring her pleasure, and he follows through for the next ten minutes. Even if he thinks he knows, she should still direct him on where and how to touch her and kiss her.

Then you alternate; he lies down on the bed and she caresses him all over his body (except the genitals) for five minutes, saying loving things to him as she did the night before. Then he leads her by telling her what he'd like her to do to bring him pleasure, and she follows through for ten minutes.

Neither of you should reach orgasm at this time, so stop short and tell your partner to do something else if you come close.

Next, he focuses as much time on her as it takes to get her close to orgasm. At that point, he enters her. Both of you say, "I love you," or make some other loving comment at least once during intercourse. He can slow his movements in order to prolong his time before orgasm, but she should tell him when she is very close to orgasm, at which point he can orgasm as well.

If your partner does not reach orgasm, then bring him or her to orgasm after intercourse using whatever method your partner would like.

As a reminder, no partner should feel pressure to participate in any sexual contact that is either painful or humiliating. If you have questions about this or disagree about whether an act should be considered humiliating, consult a mental health professional.

Monday

Appreciate (Time commitment: A few minutes each day). Call on the phone, text, e-mail, or say in person while looking in your partner's eyes a statement of love and two things you appreciate about him or her. Do this every day from now on.

Enjoy silent talk night (Time commitment: Fifty minutes). Most people who need to reconnect have had some unfortunate history together. Clearly, to move on there needs to be some resolution about it. Usually, though, discussions quickly turn into fighting and finger pointing. Tonight you'll broach some of the tougher issues, but you'll do it using your new listening skills. And you won't utter a word, not right away at least. Instead you'll write down what you want to say, taking the chance to consider your feelings and responses. Each of you should bring up a minimum of one issue and a maximum of two (if time permits). You start by writing your issue, saying it out loud, and then passing the paper to your partner who then writes a response and reads it to you. You each continue to respond in writing, then reading it aloud and passing the paper back and forth until you feel you've said what you needed to. Whoever goes first has a maximum of twenty minutes for this process.

Only share after you've given it some thought and taken time to write down everything you want to say. Do not talk impulsively, and do not share anything you feel is not pressing or can wait. Do your best *not* to go far back in history and try to only discuss situations that are recent. For example, if your partner embarrassed you in some manner last week, just discuss that one incident instead of bringing up the other examples from the past few years.

After the twenty minutes of writing and talking about any topic, stop discussing it and work on forming some plan of resolution in the next five minutes. The partner who has somehow offended or hurt the other suggests some way to avoid doing it again in the future. The partner who was offended can also offer suggestions. Everything must be written down first before speaking.

After the first twenty-five minutes have elapsed, it's your partner's turn to start an issue. If each of you takes less than the suggested twenty minutes per issue, you can go back and forth for one more issue per person.

You can take turns as needed for fifty minutes. If you have each discussed two issues and you still have time left over, spend the rest of your time catching up on your day. Stop anyway at the fifty-minute mark, even if you need more time. If you haven't resolved anything or you don't feel better by then, spending more time is much more likely to incite a fight than solve a problem. You will have time to redo or discuss other matters next time.

Relax (Time commitment: Thirty minutes). After your talk, resist the urge to stay upset or feel like you're left hanging. Commit to spending time with each other, preferably cuddling. If you do not feel like talking much then (and this is the only time you can use your time this way) watch a television show, preferably something light and comical.

Tuesday

Explore the past (Time commitment: Forty-five minutes). Each partner asks the other person the following questions. The other partner answers aloud, and the first partner uses the listening skills described on page 158 to respond.

- What is one of your happiest childhood memories?
- What is one of your saddest childhood memories?
- Who was your closest childhood friend?
- Did you remember ever thinking how you wanted to do things differently when you were an adult? If so, in what way? Do you feel you've accomplished this?
- How do you think your childhood has affected how you live your adult life in a positive way?
- How do you think your childhood has affected how you live your adult life in a negative way?
- How would you like our relationship to be similar to your parents' relationship?
- How would you like our relationship to be different from your parents' relationship?
- Who was there for you when you were growing up?
- How can I be there for you more?

Make love (Time commitment: Thirty minutes). Take five minutes for slowly touching each other. Refer to Sunday's instructions. Or if you prefer, each partner can pleasure the other to orgasm. If you choose the latter option, then he pleasures her first.

Wednesday

Deal with life (Time commitment: Thirty minutes). Use this time to discuss any issues of daily life that need to be dealt with, or decisions that need to be made, whether financial, child-related, or any other problems you need to manage. At the end of this time either make the decisions you need to or at least plan who's going to follow up to get these issues closer to resolution. If thirty minutes isn't enough time, stop anyway and add another thirty minutes tomorrow night.

Relax and connect (Time commitment: Forty-five minutes). Relax with each other. Have a drink, listen to music, exchange massages, play a board game, take a walk or drive, get some tea or coffee. Read to each other. Share some funny moments of the day.

Thursday

Relax and connect (Time commitment: Forty-five minutes). Refer to Wednesday's instructions.

Make love (Time commitment: Thirty to forty-five minutes). Refer to Tuesday's instructions.

Friday

Enjoy toast night (Time commitment: Thirty minutes). With champagne or sparkling cider, toast each other on reconnecting this past week. Share with each other:

1. Your favorite parts of the week
2. The hardest part for you
3. What you were most surprised about
4. Why you want to repeat this week all over again

Week Two

Repeat week one with a few minor changes:

Friday night: After toasting each other, repeat the appreciation exercise, adding one new appreciative comment. (Remember that you should have been sending loving and appreciative messages every day.)

Saturday night: *After* your sexual desire building, you can choose to have sex.

Sunday: This time the wife plans Turn Back Time night.

After week two is over, meet in order to decide how you both want to plan the next week. Perhaps you do not have as much time every day to spend together as you did for these two weeks (although I do not think 11½ hours was an outrageous amount of time out of 168 hours in a week). You both still need to commit to an agreed amount of time and continue to implement the parts of the reconnection program that have been working for you.

Congratulations! You've proven to yourselves that when you really take the time to focus on being in love with each other, your relationship can work for both of you. Now take that renewed energy and remember how good it feels so that you can inspire each other to make future plans about creating an atmosphere of love in your everyday life.

9

Always Be Honest

Lying is hazardous to any relationship and is one of the hardest mistakes to overcome. We depend on some collective form of reality, and when a partner gazes into the eyes of someone he or she claims to love and lies, it calls into question the validity of the connection. Lying is about both the words we say and the deceit involved when we choose not to discuss things we may do that our spouses would deem inappropriate. People who are cheated on readily say the lying and deception were almost as damaging as the cheating itself. Developing honesty in your relationship will not only protect you from cheating, it will allow you to trust each other, which is a primal need to create a close, loving relationship.

Of course, lying and deceit are logical and necessary precursors to cheating. As with men who cheated in my previous study, women lied a great deal about their infidelity. I had one conversation with Oprah in which she expressed the belief that more female than male cheaters would confess. She was right—14 percent of women told their husbands about the cheating without being asked, compared to only 7 percent of men. Twice as many women confessed than men. But all told, many more women did not tell, compared with those who did tell. Sixty-two percent of cheating women have yet to disclose their cheating ways. Specifically, 38 percent have never been questioned and have been tight-lipped about it, and 24 percent lied to their husbands even after they had discovered some evidence of a relationship (but not hard evidence of actual sex). Sixteen percent did confess after their husbands had evidence.

What is really curious is that only 5 percent told their husbands after the first time they were questioned, and only 3 percent told after their husbands questioned them multiple times. In my research into cheating husbands, 12 percent of men told after first being questioned, and 12 percent told after being questioned multiple times. One thing is clear: asking a cheating woman if she's cheating is a waste of breath. Only 8 percent of women will tell compared to 24 percent of men who will tell under similar circumstances.

Often the faithful partners feel something in the gut, have noticed little details that don't quite add up, and are on the lookout for discrepancies in their partner's stories. When the outright lies come forward, they can't imagine that someone could lie so well, right to their face, and it causes them to pause and start considering sometimes absurd tales to explain otherwise obvious circumstances.

We all want to believe our partners. We deeply want to trust, and we are deeply hurt when that trust is taken advantage of. It also creates a problem for being able to heal and advance the relationship after the cheating is out in the open. After discovering a partner's infidelity, almost every person who's willing to consider staying married asks, "How will I trust? My partner told me many times that there was nothing going on, so now when I hear that, it means nothing." As you may know from *The Truth about Cheating*, I've gone so far as to enlist the help of lie detector tests to help put partners' minds at ease or to force a cheater to come clean and stop the lies.

This book is not about helping you catch a cheating partner. It is about learning from the suffering and mistakes of others so that you can create a better relationship for yourself and your mate. Lying has little place in relationships and every couple should actively work to diminish it. If your marriage already exists in an atmosphere of permissible lying, could it lead to more serious lying? Most probably. I don't mean that a partner won't cheat if there's been no lying in the past, but I've discovered something crucial from this research and my experience.

If a husband and wife have a serious commitment to honesty, it dramatically reduces the chances of either one of them cheating. The less that the lines of truth are blurred, the harder it becomes to cheat. If two people are seriously committed to honesty and develop a history of that, it does become harder for either of them to suddenly turn into a good liar. It also keeps a potential cheater thinking that he or she won't be able to get away with cheating, even if the temptation is there. If one partner begins to flirt with the idea of cheating, the other partner will pick up on something going on before it gets too far, because of the honesty that the two of them have developed. When that partner asks why the other isn't answering her cell phone as much, why he's returning home later, why he isn't as into sex . . . it'll be harder for the other to lie if they've maintained a culture of of honesty in their marriage.

But when it becomes acceptable to lie about almost everything, it sets a precedent and surely makes it easier to lie and easier to cheat. A wife may be thinking, "C'mon, if my husband is going to cheat, it's going to happen, and being honest about whether he was with that friend I can't stand last night at the game won't make the difference." Wrong. Cheaters aren't simply bad people who'll cheat no matter what. Remember, the women and men in my research felt guilty, and many wished in the end that they'd never cheated. The success of your relationship has everything to do with protecting your relationship. Lying, deceitfulness, and not correcting misinformation seeds fertile soil for gross lies and deceit.

To rebuild your relationship, it is essential to institute a no-lie policy. No-lie policies are struggles for every one of us, because we all lie. When a woman asks her partner if any part of her looks big in that outfit, he'd better say "Not at all" or else the night is over. If a man drives up with his new car (that he discussed with his partner before purchasing) and the color is not her first choice, she'd better say "Fantastic" or else she'll hear about it forever. So with all of this anticipated, diplomatic lying going on, where do we draw the line? Consider making this simple, yet necessary distinction:

Lies I can live with

Lies I cannot live with

I help couples use a policy I refer to as "action/inaction honesty." It means that at the very least, there will be complete honesty regarding any action taken, or any inaction. If you ask your wife if she made the deposit and she didn't, that's an *inaction* and she has got to be straight up front with you. If you ask your husband if he went out with a good friend whom you hate and have asked him to not go out with, he has got to be honest and tell you the truth, as that is an *action* taken. This policy also means that actions and inactions must be offered up, even if they have not been asked about, if either of you knows the other might be concerned. So even if you have no clue that your husband spent time with the friend you hate, he must tell you. This concept of sharing and dealing with the issue instead of sweeping it under the rug will force your relationship to deal with the truth. Stop hiding stuff that both of you know the other partner would disapprove of or be disappointed about. As difficult as the truth is, it beats reality distortion hands down, and it gives you the opportunity to deal with the real issue. If you really feel the friend you hate is evil incarnate and is dangerous to your husband or your relationship, deal with it. You may have to accept that things aren't always as you want them to be, but at least you'll know the truth and be able to deal with it as you wish. Obviously, the policy applies to both of you in the same way.

This policy allows lies about opinions, such as: How do I look? What do you think of my mother? Questions that we hope we can be honest about, but in the reality of life it might be more sensible to compromise the truth with little white lies. But this kind of lying is distinctly different from lying about something you did or did not concretely do. When you lie about an opinion, you don't distort reality nearly the same way as when you lie about an action or inaction. Your partner knows it's an *opinion* to start with, and therefore a lot is left to your personal judgment, which can even change with time. Ask me if I liked the outfit, maybe I didn't when I first saw it and an hour later, I liked it.

An important amendment to this rule is that either of you is allowed to not answer when it comes only to an opinion. For example, "I don't want to talk about my opinion of your mother. I'll be nice to her and it'll help if we do this." And perhaps no one should be asking for an opinion on how something looks unless they are prepared to hear an honest opinion. If you're fishing for a compliment, tell your partner outright, "I love it when you compliment how I look when I get dressed up to go out for the evening," or, "I always dreamed of owning this type of car and want you to be happy about it for me."

My research has shown that it is highly unlikely for women or men to admit to cheating, period. It's worth every effort to develop a relationship that is surrounded by honesty in all parts of your life. An honest relationship will likely diminish the odds of cheating, and surely will allow you to take notice quicker and easier if your partner is pulling away emotionally or physically. It will help you discover the truth earlier on about your partner's dissatisfaction with the relationship or deceitful actions, possibly avoiding irreparable damage. You'll be able to see if your partner is telling the truth, because there aren't lies always being bandied about. Both of you can commit to having a relationship in which both partners can be honest, even if you know it may upset the other person. It will also cut down on doing things that upset each other because they can't be hidden so easily. Bringing issues out in the open is the one thing we've learned needs to happen. It's what cheating and faithful women know for sure they need in their marriages: more open, honest communication. Now you'll know what's really going on in your partner's life, which allows both of you to deal with your issues together instead of waiting until they get out of hand. Being able to trust your partner is a prerequisite to ongoing understanding and sensitivity to each other. Everyone needs to be heard and deserves a partner who makes a consistent effort to truly listen.

PART THREE

Connecting to Love
for Good

10

How to Make Real Changes That Last

As you've read this book, you've probably had all kinds of reactions to different points, and you'll want to have a deeper understanding of those reactions especially if they were negative enough that you know you're not going to follow through with the suggestions. The point of this chapter is to help you identify what provokes some of these ticks and what you can do to change the impulses and feelings that simply are not working for you or your partner in this relationship.

I've been asked many times if I get tired or depressed doing what I do, listening to the pain and hurt of others. Whereas admittedly it can be tiring and intensely stressful to be in the moment with others as they journey through complicated and often painful feelings and experiences, I am always inspired throughout. This inspiration comes from every person with whom I experience genuine change. Our ability to change, as I said in the introduction, is what makes us human.

We have an incredible ability to make wonderful lasting changes in our lives. Many people don't want to believe it—they might be concerned about the work involved to make such changes, or they truly haven't found the way to do it. There are many who want to make changes, but they have become prisoners to their impulses and can control them only to a point for a short while. People don't change not because they don't want to, but because they don't know how. Most follow the commonsense approach of just reminding themselves of what needs to be done and using sheer willpower—do what you have to do. This is workable for some issues that are mild and will work for major issues for some time, but it misses a vital component of real change.

I know that people can change because I have seen it, time and time again, in my twenty-three years of counseling couples whose marriages are in trouble. And it's not just their outward behavior that changes. It's their fundamental feelings inside—how they feel about themselves as well as their partners. They come to counseling to see if their marriage can be saved. But in a very short time, they discover the deeper reasons why they act the way they do. They begin to understand themselves *and* their partners. Their motivation to do things differently comes from within, rather than from a list of rules and procedures imposed from the outside. Anyone can begin a new journey to turn a relationship around.

Almost every couple that comes to me has at least one partner who believes that there is no hope because people don't change.

I explain that often it's not the personality that needs changing. People confuse personality with the "internal processor," the voice inside that directs the different parts of one's personality and history. If your partner is the life of the party and loves attention, you might not need that to change. Being the life of the party is not what caused him or her to cheat on you, ignore you, or be insensitive to you. There are many life-of-the-party personalities who do nothing of the sort.

This chapter discusses some of those inner voices and other aspects deep inside us that cause us to act in ways we don't like or understand. And it offers some true and clear examples of people just like you who found the strength—and more important, the personal understanding—to make healthy, substantive changes that stuck.

Changes That Are Good for You

Often husbands and wives find the will to change because they have done something to hurt their partners. One of them will ask the other one to change, even sometimes when the couple is yet unsure if the relationship will continue. Maybe you've hurt your partner so much that you could change in every way requested and there's still no guarantee that you'll stay together. Why work so hard, you may ask yourself, to create change in yourself if you don't even know you'll stay with the person that you're changing for?

But you are not just changing for your partner. Although the catalyst for any change may well be your partner's request, the change will benefit you no matter what. I've rarely heard a partner request that his or her mate change, where it wouldn't be a good thing for that person to change regardless of whether the couple remains together. Yes, perhaps you'd never make these changes if you weren't in this relationship. Perhaps another partner would be okay with this behavior you're being asked to change. But if you believe that making the change itself would be good for you anyway, then you are doing it for yourself ultimately to grow into a better human being, in addition to attempting to right a wrong or make your partner happy.

Often, by the time a couple is in trouble, they have talked a great deal about their problems. Typically, there have been suggestions for change, and promises for change, as well as periods when there was change. But things often settle back into the same old pattern, and partners begin to believe that change won't stick. Sometimes one partner believes that the other person really doesn't want to change, and that's why the failure continues. I caution couples about this because I truly believe that people are often not given the information they need to create real change. But what any offending partner must realize is that it is not enough to promise change for your partner to want to continue to be open to loving you, even when the promise comes with great remorse.

Let's take cheating as an example. If you have had an affair, and now you are remorseful and swear to never do it again, you can't understand why that promise isn't enough. After all, you wonder, what else can you do? The problem is that your partner assumes that you thought it was wrong to cheat before you cheated as well. Over 80 percent of men and women who cheated never thought they'd cheat when they were first married. So you already had this belief system in your mind and you still cheated. What's to say you won't do it again? You might suggest that you see now how wrong it is and how much it hurt your partner. But you now want your partner not only to stay with you but to be emotionally vulnerable to you. How can your partner entrust that vulnerability to you when he or she believes there is an increased chance of feeling stabbed in the back if you cheat again?

The answer is that it isn't enough to feel bad and swear fidelity. You've got to discover what inside you put you in the place to hurt your loved one and risk your couplehood and family. What stopped you from doing things differently, even if that meant discussing change seriously in your relationship so that you felt no desire to cheat? You had so many options, yet you took one that caused unimaginable pain. So asking your partner to become vulnerable again and just get over it isn't workable. But if you can discover something new about yourself, attain a deeper understanding of what makes you do things that could hurt your partner, you will have the strength and foresight to make new changes. Then your partner can see that you're not just going to "control" yourself, you're going to make changes so there won't be a struggle within that you're actively fighting. Your partner will see that how you treat your relationship has changed, and there will develop a closeness within your relationship that makes you even closer than you might have been before the affair.

Our Many Voices Within

Our brains protect us from traumatic situations by relieving us of our thoughts. Each of us has three voices in our head that help us to process these thoughts: the child voice, the society voice, and the home voice. In my book *The Truth about Cheating,* I describe each of the voices in more detail; together they comprise what I call my Inner Voice Recognition Formula, which is a tool I use to help you dissect the subtle ways in which your brain processes major issues. If you haven't already, please review the chapter in that book to learn about the society and home voices, because I do not discuss them fully here. Instead I want to go into greater detail about the primary voice, the child voice, to help you develop an understanding of yourself so you can create substantive changes in how you work in your relationship.

Our speaking voice frequently changes, although we don't always hear it ourselves. A friend might clue us in by saying, "What's wrong? It sounds like you're sick." If we're happy or sad, awake or tired, it'll directly affect our communication pattern. And we don't even realize it. If that's what's happening on the outside, where we can physically hear ourselves, imagine what's happening on the inside. Indeed, we have many voices within clamoring to speak; and depending on many different factors, a specific voice will get first billing and lead us on our way. The problem is, when this happens we call it our "reaction," as though it just is and there's not much we can do about it. That's where we are all dead wrong. We can begin to learn which voices we use when different situations come our way.

The Context of Childhood

Even though the exact science regarding nature versus nurture is inconclusive, we can be sure that our childhood is a major factor in how we become who we are. When we are little beings, we have no choice but to accept the messages around us as truths, whether these messages serve our best interests or not. Of all the messages we receive and swallow hook, line, and sinker, an overwhelming number have little to do with truth at all.

Take a simple example of a child who brings her parent a Mother's or Father's Day present she made in kindergarten. (In my day we frequently used papier-mâché, which we typically formed into an ashtray regardless of whether our parents smoked.) The child busies herself creating some new misshapen object that she artistically paints in beautiful harmonic colors—

green and orange—and presents it with pride. The child hopes for the obvious perfect response from the parent. "You made this? I can't believe it. It's beautiful," and the child walks away feeling on top of the world. Remarkably, this feeling is not based on an objective truth. The child made something worthless that couldn't be given away for free to the neighbor and the only reason she created it in the first place was that a teacher instructed her to do so. Yet, the stage is set and that child is made to believe something about her is absolutely wonderful.

Equally affecting would be for the parent to get the present and look bewildered, commenting, "Well, it's nice and all but I don't smoke and I'm not sure where it would go." The child receiving that response would be heartbroken—and again, it has little to do with the object made and everything to do with the message the parent chooses to send at that moment.

I don't believe that one comment or the other is going to make or break a child's emotional well-being for the rest of her life. However, millions of comments, actions, and inactions in one direction or the other will. Our parents gave us message after message about life at a time when we had no choice but to accept their opinion as the law of life. Often, they intended only to help us, but it doesn't mean they always did.

What could a five-year-old possibly think if his parent tells him he's bad for making his mom cry by telling her he hates her? The child feels rotten and guilty, and never once does it dawn on him that perhaps his mom has a depressive disorder or some emotionally fragile issue that would cause her to take to heart her five-year-old child's comment, instead of realizing that it's an acting-out moment and that she needs to teach her son how to properly express anger. What else could a five-year-old think when he's lavished with hugs and kisses from his mom "just because," other than that he must be the best kid in the world, instead of realizing that his mom is an upbeat, passionate woman with high energy to love anyone who would've been her child.

Young children don't understand the why behind events, but are prisoners to whatever message is sent as a complete truth. As we just saw, it can work either in their favor or to their detriment. But it all has so little to do with the child and so much more to do with the child's parents. Typically, parents want what is best for their children. They don't stay up late at night trying to figure out how to make their children sad and stressed, but life happens. Bad marriages happen. Economic downturns happen. Postpartum depression happens, as do illness and other forms of family loss. Parents do their best with what they have, but the roller coaster of life can cause reactions in them that may not send stellar, positive messages to their children. Unfortunately, children take every-thing personally as though each event is describing them. If a parent is depressed for an extended period of time, a child learns that life is to be lived that way. When the child laughs and the par-ent does not smile back, the child learns that she should not be laughing or she is not worthy of such behavior. It doesn't need to be said by the parent, and it probably isn't even meant to be taught by the parent, but it is the reality of that child for that period of time.

Children absorb everything around them. By the time a person is twelve years old, she's largely formed an image of herself that will stay with her for the rest of her life. Many psychologists bring that number way down to six years old. Ask any first grade teacher who's been at it for a while, and she'll tell you that however a kid is in first grade is pretty much how that kid will be as an adult. If in first grade the child was sweet or difficult, outgoing or intro-verted, studious or athletic, easygoing or highly stressed, the child will carry the same traits as an adult. People often mistakenly explain that they were largely formed by their adolescence, but what they may be missing is that by the time they reached their teenage years, they were already acting on the beliefs they held about themselves as kids. There was already a personal belief system in place that they carried into adolescence. They already viewed life through the messages they were given about themselves, whether given directly from their parents' words, or from their nonverbal cues or their inaction.

I am not saying that kids never change, but usually it takes something extreme in life or some form of real therapy or otherwise focused attempt to change. You can have a very outgoing girl at seven who is molested and then becomes an introverted teen, just as you can have a very shy child whose parents win the lottery and travel the world with her, turning her into an extroverted, confident teen. But typically, how we get out of the starting gate as little kids is where we often end up, because our parents usually reinforce those messages throughout our upbringing. If your parents lavished you with love and praise by the time you were seven, they probably continued doing the same throughout your upbringing; the same would be assumed if they treated you negatively at times.

Of course, most childhoods are not all good or all bad, so it's not easy to just find out what message you received and work with it. But make no mistake that what happened to you and me as children set us both up for life. It created a belief system on so many levels that it is the number one place you should be looking to understand yourself and make a change. The fact that childhood has a powerful impact is not often disputed. But no one likes to return to childhood and think about the pain or sadness. People rationalize their reluctance to really think about childhood by saying that it happened long ago so why go back there; and it can't be used as an excuse for their actions later in life. Quite so.

Let me be clear. *I am not asking you to judge your parents.* You cannot do that, nor can anyone else, because in order to do so we'd have to know everything about how they grew up and all of their challenges. If a child was badly beaten as a youth and he grows up to care for his own children, never hits them, but is never very loving toward them either, perhaps that man is considered a wonderful success in the scheme of life. Only God knows, literally. However, I'm asking you to forget about judgment and focus on *impact*. Your parents' actions and beliefs had an impact on how you came to feel about yourself. That's what we're after here—understanding the effects of your childhood relationships.

If you have any question about the power of childhood, take an example that has nothing to do with parents. Take someone who at age fifty becomes terrified when a tiny Yorkie dog licks his ankle in a mall. Perhaps he starts screaming at the owner. Yet, if he was chased and bitten by a Rottweiler when he was six, he may have been implanted with a fear of dogs that is now illogical. But as his heart races and beads of sweat form, someone telling him not to be afraid is not much help. We all can change but it'll take work, because once we get something into our heads as kids, it sticks like glue (or papier-mâché). There is a stimulus, in this case the dog, and a response, fear. Stimulus and response. They form early from our experiences on the planet.

When people tell me they don't want to blame their childhoods, they imply that they're going to find out something about their past that is somehow going to excuse their behavior. Understanding why you do what you do doesn't excuse it; it just gives you a way to change it. But to avoid looking at your childhood is to avoid a deeper understanding of who you are and why you may behave the way you do. In the examples to come, you'll see how childhood can directly correlate to our adult lives.

Exercise: Start Understanding Your Childhood

Your Relationship with Your Parent of the Opposite Sex

Consider your relationship with your parent of the opposite sex. We tend to expect our adult love relationships to be similar to our relationship with that parent. Rate that parent in each of the categories below, using a scale of 1 to 5 (1 = "not at all"; 5 = "very much").

My opposite-sex parent:

Was touchy/feely (physically demonstrating emotion).

Was verbally kind.

Was physically present.

Made me feel good.

Really understood me.

Made me feel bad.

Was mean.

Was unkind.

Was neglectful.

Spent time with me.

Laughed with me.

List at least three (more if they come easily) strong memories of something you experienced with this parent, good or bad, from your youth (under age twelve).

How My Parents Made Me Feel in General about Myself

Now consider how both parents made you feel about yourself. Did they instill in you a sense of love, confidence, and warmth, or more of a sense of being unworthy, neglected, and alone? Rate your parents in each of the categories below, using a scale of 1 to 5 (1 = "not at all"; 5 = "very much").

My parents made me feel:

Proud

Loved

Worthy

Unworthy

Capable

Confident

Weird

Ill fitting

Lonely

Connected to family

Connected to community

Smart

Stupid

My Parents' Relationship

Finally, consider your impression of your parents' marriage or relationship. What did it model for you about how relationships work? Rate your parents in each category, using a scale of 1 to 5 (1 = "not at all"; 5 = "very much").

Toward each other, they were

Loving

Fighting

Complimentary

Appreciative

Diminishing

Humiliating

Warm

Physically demonstrative (in front of me)

Helpful

List at least three (more if they come easily) strong memories, good or bad, of the way your parents related to each other from your youth (under age twelve).

What do you do with this information? First, reflect on how these memories could have impacted you personally as far as how you see your life today. Next, consider how your relationship with your partner may have similarities to your relationship as a child with your opposite-sex parent, as well as if your adult love relationship is similar to your parents' relationship. Keep in mind that we're discussing feelings, not making exact comparisons. You may have had a dad who was unsuccessful as a provider and a husband who is a high-powered businessman. But let's say your dad was always complaining about his work or lack thereof. Though he may be very successful, your husband can still complain the same amount. Maybe your dad hit you a lot and your husband doesn't, but your husband puts you down in front of others, making you feel very much the same way your dad did when he hit you. There are connections there.

Perhaps your mom was aggressive and screamed about how everything you did was wrong. Your wife may be extremely quiet and unhappy; nothing you do seems to make her anything but depressed, so you continue to feel that nothing you do is right—just as you did when you were a child. There's your connection. These similarities have nothing to do with your partner and opposite-sex parent looking alike or being the same personality type. It's all about how you end up feeling around that partner and how that taps into the feelings of youth.

This is not to blame your partner, but to recognize if there is something you can or cannot do to affect the behavior in your partner that is driving you to the point of feeling as you did when you were a child.

Remember, of course, that this entire theory works in a positive direction as well. If your opposite-sex parent largely made you feel loved and competent, you're much more likely to naturally find a mate who gives you the same feelings as well, even though your partner may not resemble your parent much otherwise.

The stories in this chapter are excellent examples of how understanding your deeper self can play a direct role in your adult love relationship.

Cynthia and William's Story: Fighting Constantly

By the time Cynthia and William came to me, they had already spent years fighting and were convinced they'd have no choice but to divorce. Cynthia bitterly complained that William had been neglecting her and the kids for years. She also complained that he spent too much time watching sports and not nearly enough time working. She felt he was failing the family by not being absorbed enough in the doughnut business he'd begun, even though he'd be considered a success by most standards.

William explained that when he was home, his wife was never into him and she had something to say about anything he did with the kids, like "Don't rile them up," "Can't you read to them instead of just horsing around?" or "You leave all the discipline to me." He felt that all she ever wanted from him was money. She didn't approve of him. She didn't respect him. How could he be with a woman who didn't respect him? She said she wasn't a spendthrift and didn't care about the money, but at least he should work hard enough to secure his children's future. He'd had it, and he was candid in saying that for years he'd been hiding from her with his sports interests and spending as much time away as possible.

Now, what could I tell them as a therapist? "Hey, be nicer to each other. You, work a little harder; you, stop telling him how to spend his time around the kids." That's nonsense. Do I think these two intelligent people haven't figured that answer out? Obviously, something compels them to see the issues in their own way, and that's where I could help them. I went through the exercises explained earlier in this chapter to get each of them discovering how their childhoods affected them and directly affected their relationship. Of course, there was a lot more history than what I'll provide here, but I'll focus on the primary childhood issues that spoke to the problems we've described.

William found it hard to believe that his childhood had anything to do with his wife's putting him down and not respecting him. But in the interest of humoring me, he said bluntly, "My mom was a depressed drunk." His dad left when he was little, never to be heard from again. His mother never got over her husband's abrupt exit from her life, using it as an excuse for a lifelong alcohol problem. William and his older sister raised themselves and became quite independent as young as he could remember, because they had no other choice. He had always been attracted to strong women, such as Cynthia, and he loved the capable manner in which she raised the kids and cared for the home.

Now, here was the translation of how his childhood and relationship with his mother or lack thereof was driving his part of the relationship. Internally, he had made a decision that he'd never

marry someone like his mom. She was weak, depressed, and inca-
pacitated by her drinking. But when he married Cynthia, he ended
up marrying someone who would make him feel the same way
his mother made him feel: lonely. Because she was so independent, they fell into a trap of not needing each other and being distant. He became lonely in a different way. Not because his wife
was weak like his mother, but rather, because she was strong
enough to carry on a life without him, just like his mother. In the
clever way that the brain has of replicating the familiar without us
realizing it, William's brain was helping him create a home environment of loneliness that was reminiscent of his childhood.

Remarkably, instead of trying to deal with this loneliness by
doing the logical thing and getting more involved in his family,
William decided to move farther away from his family, though in
a much milder way than his dad had. But still, just as his dad left
his mom, William emotionally left his wife, and she complained
about it just like his mom complained and blamed his dad for all
of her troubles. In that hidden brain agenda sort of way, he got his
present-day family awfully close to his childhood one. Even
though the facts were different, the feelings were quite similar.

Add to this the disrespect. Remember that William couldn't see
living with a woman who didn't approve of and respect him.
Cynthia said she respected him greatly but still needed him to do
more. But how had William felt when his mother neglected him—
dare we say the childhood version of disapproved of, or disre-
spected? Keep in mind that when William was six and under, he
must've taken his mom's neglect very personally. It wasn't until he
was about ten that he realized there was something quite different about his mom. "I thought all mothers had vodka with breakfast," he says now. So what happens to a boy whose mom chooses
not to care for him? He gets hurt and angry. William was not in
touch with his anger at his mom, nor did he want to start. But he

could see how he'd overreact to his wife's disapproval when, he came to realize, he was pushing the envelope, doing things that he knew would annoy or even infuriate her. It was his way of getting back at her for neglecting him—the "her" really being his mother.

Can it be that he was still reacting to his mother's behavior after all these years? Sure it can, and he'd been hiding from it but still reacting to it in so many ways by driving his marriage to this lonely, angry place. The proof was in his changes. When he could see how these puzzle pieces fit together, he immediately, even in my office, began to feel differently about his wife. He was comfortable, even relieved to take responsibility for his behavior of emotionally hiding from the family and blaming Cynthia for a disapproval that he now understood came in part from his unwillingness to listen to her and make any changes at all.

But there is more to the story. Cynthia came to adulthood with her own issues from childhood as well. Her dad was never around when she was a child. He worked as a train conductor and in order to earn income for his seven children, he rarely stopped working. Wherever and whenever he could go, he went, and it meant he rarely slept at home. Cynthia had a memory of her mom waking her and her siblings one night, telling them to get up quickly and see her dad, who had been gone awhile. She remembered standing at the station and watching him pass and wave at her. (We assumed that he stopped the train at the station and had a moment to get off and say hello to the family, but Cynthia didn't remember.)

It's easy to see why Cynthia learned to be quite independent of her dad. She couldn't need his love and affection because it wasn't going to be there. Her mom took care of her and all of the kids but was down on her husband for never spending enough time at home. The one thing she always told her kids that was great about her dad was the same thing she complained about: he was a very hard worker and a good provider. The love that Cynthia did receive from her dad was not the warmth of hugs and kisses but the knowledge that he was spending his life working hard to provide for her.

In her relationship, she struggled with her partner as she struggled with her dad. She wanted him to love her in a way that her dad never had, but she was stuck on her husband's work ethic as a sign of that love more than anything else. William was doing well in his doughnut business and was receiving solid money and great accolades. Could he have worked more? I suppose. But it did seem like he was working hard enough to still have this successful business. Cynthia was projecting her dad's form of love, workaholism, onto her partner and being angry with him for failing to show his love through working endlessly. She was also plain mad if he spent any nonwork time not attending to the children, another angry feeling she was borrowing from anger at her dad for not being there for her childhood.

As with most couples in trouble, their issues seemed to dovetail with each other's. They both had had difficulty being close to their opposite-sex parents, so they came to their adult relationship with serious limitations in having a healthy love for each other. They both had felt terribly lonely in childhood with regard to their opposite-sex parent, and they did things that they did not realize to make themselves lonely from their partners today. He complained about her disapproval (he grew up feeling his mom's disapproval) and was quick to step away and become distant (as he felt estranged from his mom as well). She was unconsciously angry at her dad for being distant, and turned that anger and disapproval onto her husband. She interpreted love as her husband's work ethic, and no amount of work would please her.

The problem is that when we are unaware of our childhood issues, we try to make up for pains of our past, and sadly it doesn't work. No matter how loving Cynthia would've been, William would have found ways to be upset and distant. He'd continue trying to get his mom to approve of him by testing Cynthia's resolve as he pushed her away more and more. Cynthia was so hurt by her dad's absence, and she felt guilty about it. After all, he was working for them, but that didn't take away the fact that she felt hurt and alone. No matter how much wealth William would ever generate, Cynthia was still going to be unhappy unless he worked endlessly as a way of making her feel that safe, loved feeling her dad had given her in childhood. No matter what he did with the kids, she'd find fault because deep down, she was still mad at her dad for not being there and connecting to her.

Unfortunately, we can't make the pains of our past go away by plastering them all over our adult love relationships. We keep trying to master those painful feelings of youth by driving our lives to the same harmful feelings and experiencing them again and again. The primary way of stopping the cycle is to recognize what you're doing and deal with the sadness directly as an adult. It's strange to imagine that there is this voice within that is dictating some of your negative impulses (just as there are positive ones as well). It's up to you to decide if you want to follow this feeling and belief about yourself, or if you want to face it head-on and release anyone today like your partner who's getting entangled with that voice.

Cynthia and William were reacting in harsh ways to otherwise easily resolvable issues because of the childhoods they each had experienced. Once they allowed themselves to see how their past was affecting them, they could choose to create a new adult voice that suited them in their relationship. Cynthia could create a voice that said if William is making good money, then why would she want him to be overworked and use up his life's energy in that way? If he plays with his children, how wonderful for him and their kids for that relationship to be close. Sure, he needed to be more involved in schoolwork and discipline, but now he'd be willing to make those changes as well. William could feel himself change as he no longer wanted to play out his relationship with his mom within his adult relationship with Cynthia. He didn't want to follow the voice that told him to expect and deserve loneliness and distance from the one he wanted love from the most. He could get more involved as a real dad with his kids and form a real parental team with Cynthia.

Points: Valid; Intense Reaction: Invalid

Often, the way you can see that there's something going on within you, something that you're bringing to the table, is by being really honest with yourself about your reaction to your partner. Usually, partners have valid points to make about the other person's behaviors. Cynthia's point that William wasn't involved in disciplining or schooling the kids was valid. William's point that Cynthia wanted him to work harder even though he was successful was valid. But how they each chose to react—the intensity was not commensurate with the issue. Each screamed and yelled over the issues. They both distanced themselves sharply. They took positions that didn't fit with the concept of a working family. They both loved their kids and said they meant the world to them, yet they were willing to destroy their parental relationship in front of those same kids they loved dearly.

When you are having a reaction that is intense, immediately check yourself against the voice of your past. You can see that even if your point is valid, the emotion that is being conjured up may be well out of proportion for the situation. If that is so, you are borrowing that emotion from another time and place. Face it, and you'll make the best change of your life.

So what do you do now with the knowledge you've found? You continue to focus on the voice of childhood so that you keep your issues in check. Cynthia and William see what they're doing daily to make sure that they are coming closer and avoiding loneliness. They each continue to discuss with the other their pasts and ways that they can avoid taking childhood issues out on each other.

Never Use Childhood Information against Your Partner

However, you must be careful never to use your knowledge of your partner's childhood as a get-out-of-jail-free card. Never— and this is crucial—use deep insightful information about the past against your partner as a way of diminishing his or her feelings. Cynthia can't look at William and say, "Oh, you're just being mad at your mom and you're taking it out on me." William obviously can never do the same. Even though you might feel it is accurate, it has the potential to do incredible harm; using such a deep vulnerability against the other person is a low blow and must be avoided. You can always at a later, calmer time, apologize for whatever your partner was upset at you about, and then quietly ask him or her to consider if the intensity of the reaction had anything to do with some of the past childhood history you've discussed. But this is as far as you can go unless your partner invites you to elaborate.

Make Concrete Changes Using Your Insight

Use this scale to help you understand the process of change we're discussing.

Unconsciously Skilled (US)

Consciously Skilled (CS)

Consciously Unskilled (CU)

Unconsciously Unskilled (UU)

The lowest stage is being Unconsciously Unskilled, which means you're making mistakes and are not even aware of it. An example is when Cynthia thought she was 100 percent right for being really mad that William didn't work hard enough. The next level up is Consciously Unskilled, as when Cynthia became aware enough of her issues to realize she was making a mistake with this intense anger and was using her unresolved issues with her father to hurt her relationship with her husband. Next, Cynthia became Consciously Skilled, when she used this insight to change her reactions and the way she saw William. Her impulses would tell her to be very angry at him and to feel hurt if he was not working hard enough for the family; but with her newfound awareness, she forced herself to be skilled, to reduce her anger at William by dealing with her anger at her dad. She could do this by writing down her feelings about her dad in a journal when she was getting angry at William, or by finding some other way to focus on this internal dialogue she needed to have. Once she did this for a while, she would arrive at the top of the scale and be Unconsciously Skilled, meaning she would no longer even be struggling within, as she truly would have changed her internal voice and dialogue, allowing her to be free from the negative issues of her childhood.

Of course, William worked through the same scale to accomplish his changes as well. He came to the discussion feeling that he was completely in the right that his wife disapproved of him and he had every right to scream and be distant. He soon allowed himself to get to CU, where he realized he didn't need to react this way and he was transferring the loneliness of his relationship and anger at his mother onto his relationship with Cynthia. He then worked hard at getting to CS, where he fought his impulse to get angry and pull away from his partner emotionally. Finally he got to US, no longer feeling the struggle to be angry often or looking for ways to leave Cynthia and be distant from her.

No book could ever give enough examples to cover your unique situation and life. But you can use this scale and the exercises laid out at the beginning of this chapter to take a major step into learning about yourself and taking responsibility for any negative intensity that you are contributing to your relationship.

Dawn and Tim's Story: Lots of Great Sex Didn't Work for Them

When Dawn came to me complaining that her husband was uninterested in having sex with her, it was surprising to hear her husband, Tim, respond with, "She's incredible in bed but I don't know why it's just not enough." It wasn't as if he was unable to be sexually aroused, as evidenced by the fact that he used pornography to achieve satisfaction alone. Dawn was unhappy that he preferred taking care of his own needs instead of having sex with her. She felt crushed and doubted her looks, her mind, and her general ability in life due to his lack of sexual desire for her. Tim knew it didn't make much sense, but what could he do? Sex just wasn't much fun for him, and as much as his wife was a very creative and competent sex partner, he felt that he could never please her. As willing as she was to get creative in making him happy, she was unwilling to let him be creative in making her happy sexually. The turn-on for him in watching porn was seeing the woman be pleased, something he felt he couldn't begin to do with his wife.

Seems pretty simple, right? Have more sex with more creativity going both ways. What's more fun than that? Except this had leaked into every part of their marriage and they had already seen divorce attorneys a year earlier, although they hadn't gone through with it. They went to not one but two sex therapists, who had given what appeared to me to be pretty good advice. But it was a great disappointment when they couldn't follow through, and the little they did ended in disaster. It sounds like a sexual problem plain and simple, but it's a mistake to reduce serious problems to their outer symptoms. Sure, the first response is always to try to resolve the problem with some behavioral changes. But when that doesn't work or people are unwilling or feel incapable of following those behavioral suggestions, it's time to look deeper. As we said, each of them had valid points, but the intensity of their hostility and hurt over the problem was extreme—maybe not now after years of suffering, but as they reported it, the hurt and anger were extreme from the outset as their sex life just began faltering. The fact that they were not able to resolve and correct their issues with some simple changes early on showed that there was something deeper going on.

As it turned out, they both had much to discover about their childhoods. Dawn's parents divorced when she was twelve, and had hated each other for years. Dawn loved her father dearly, and he sounded like an attentive, loving dad. She was devastated when he left the home and she was unable to see him much for a period of four years, since she moved with her mom out of state to be with her mom's parents. Her dad's departure still weighed heavily on her as an adult, and although she rarely thought about it, the telling of the incident brought her to tears. So much for things staying in the past. A telling incident had occurred when she was screaming as a kid at her mom, in a way blaming her for her dad leaving, at which point her mom unfortunately stated bluntly that her dad had been cheating. At that point her dad, who had been upstairs, came barreling down to yell, "Had you been giving me any sex the last year, things would've been different."

There it was. Her dad, whom she so loved, leaving her life because her mom didn't give him sex and he cheated. Within two years, her mom remarried, and it turned out her stepdad was a horrible individual who molested Dawn over a six-month period before becoming weak due to a terminal illness that caused his death within a year of the diagnosis. Dawn never told either of her parents that she had been molested. The only person she had ever told was a close college friend, until she shared it at the meeting with her husband and me.

She was a promiscuous teen, and without ever thinking it through, she became a woman who was focused on giving her man lots of wonderful sex. She lost her dad because in her mind he wasn't getting sex. Her stepfather taught her that she was nothing but a sex object. The truth was that sex was mixed with disgust, fear, and guilt largely due to the criminal activity of her stepfather, but it left her completely disgusted if her husband tried to please her sexually unless it was just part of intercourse when she could have some good physical feelings associated with it. She couldn't remember the last time she had an orgasm or if she truly ever did.

She was great at giving sex but limited at receiving it. When her husband became the slightest bit uninterested in her, or they had sex less often, she had an extreme reaction—terribly fearful that she'd lose him, and angry, very angry that they weren't having sex enough. But this was years ago when they were still having plenty of sex but not as much as they'd been having. Dawn learned that her definition was tied up in serving a man sex, both from losing her dad and then being molested. She had never put the pieces of the puzzle together, never saw it quite this way. Sure she knew her stepfather's molestation affected her, but in her mind as long as she was willing to have sex, it wasn't actively bothering her. She was wrong, and only now could she be open to it.

Naturally, her issues collided with her husband's childhood issues. Tim's parents were dispassionate. Mom served Dad, putting dinner on the table without fail at six as the newspaper lay comfortably by the side of his plate. Her life involved making Dad comfortable, but there wasn't much connection. As much as she served Tim's father, she complained to Tim bitterly for as long as Tim could remember about his dad being too close to his secretaries. There'd be some weekly fight without fail between them as Mom accused Dad of cheating with whichever secretary was working that year. There was no pleasing Mom—she suffered as a martyr in her role of caregiver and self-proclaimed servant of the household. She suffered from physical ailments, all due to her putting endless energy into serving her husband and children while not caring for her own health or well-being.

Tim realized that being served came easily to him, and that worked for a while at the start of his relationship with his wife. She was quite service-oriented, and although he should've been uncomfortable with her lack of willingness to receive sexual pleasure, he wasn't. In fact, he was thrilled because he had heard so much about his dad's possible cheating (he never verified if his father had ever actually cheated) that he never wanted to do so and figured that lots of sex would be the antidote to such concerns.

Was it a coincidence that somehow over time he ended up in a marriage as dispassionate as his parents'? Sure, it may not have looked the same, but he did his part without realizing it to drive his marriage to the same place his parents' marriage had ended up: disconnected. Even two highly sexual people can end up with a nonexistent sex life and a lousy emotional life to match. His mom served his dad; and he found a woman who loved to do the same, particularly in the sexual area, which was the primary sub-ject of arguments between his parents. When he told me about his favorite porn video, he couldn't help but openly gasp; it featured a man having sex with his secretary. In an odd sort of way, he had traded in sex with his wife for sex with a secretary, similar to the theme of his childhood and his parents' issues. It no longer came as a surprise to Tim as to why he became disenchanted with his wife's wonderful sexual giving after he had found it so great for the beginning of their relationship.

Now the two of them had become consciously unskilled. They finally opened themselves up to seeing what role each of them played in their failing marriage. Next came the step of being con-sciously skilled, focusing great energy into losing the voices of their upbringing and using a new adult voice to lead them. Dawn had her work cut out for her. It would be slow going in allowing her to stay ever present with Tim as she allowed him in small stages to please her and focus on her sexual pleasure. Sex had to become more about their partnership and less about her trying not to lose her dad and to use sex as a degrading, humiliating activity.

Tim needed to work through his familiarity and comfort with being disconnected from his wife the way his parents had been with each other. He had to stop flirting with the idea of secretary sex and focus on how much he truly loved his wife and bring that love to his sexual life, making it about sharing love. Both of them had sexual issues, so they'd need to lose the sex and find the love. They needed a lot more foreplay, much more hugging and kissing and friendship so that the sex became a flower that blossomed out of the relationship instead of the main event it used to be. Both of them chose to write about their feelings toward their parents, so that they were resolving their issues in the right place and letting them leak less and less into their marriage. Writing for your own insights is a good outlet and allows for processing of difficult issues. Dawn also wrote a letter to her deceased stepfather, telling him all the things she needed to say but never had the courage, understanding, or the chance to tell him when she was young. She would in time turn the molestation of her past completely on him and no longer harbor the unfortunate guilt and self-hatred that she had carried for years.

I know many more examples of couples who have been helped to make substantive, lasting changes as a result of focused insight into their childhoods. It is not a simple thing to accomplish, and that is largely why so many avoid trying it. And many people just don't know how, or even that there could be such connections between their childhood experiences and their adult lives today. But as these stories show, once you make the connections, you have such an increased chance of making real change that will impact your marriage immediately. You can find peace and real spiritual comfort in freeing up that space for your own life as well. It's worth every bit of effort.

11

How Women Can Communicate More Openly

Unfaithful women in my study said that the number one thing they would do differently, if they could go back to the time before they cheated, would be to "try to communicate more openly with my husband." Unhappy, faithful women agreed, as the majority of them wished they could better communicate with their husbands. Even though women often feel that they express their feelings pretty well, there is still too much of a great divide between the sexes. Communication means not just expressing yourself, but also finding the best form of expression to help your husband hear your message.

Three things usually hamper communication between women and their husbands:

- The woman not understanding her own issues clearly.

- The woman's inability to articulate her issues in a way that her husband will take them seriously.

- The man's unwillingness to consider another viewpoint.

Criticism is hard for anyone to take. In his book *How to Win Friends and Influence People*, Dale Carnegie's first rule is "never criticize." No one likes to be criticized, and it usually puts us in defense mode. When couples get into a fight, it's as if something goes off in their heads that says, "Let's throw out every piece of crap we ever have experienced in this marriage and let my partner have it all. There's never a good time to bring this up, so now's as good a time as any." All of the criticisms are expelled—more to fight about—until finally someone runs out of steam. But the issues are never truly discussed or resolved. There is no calm forum when the partners have each other's attention. Nothing is done to soften the blow of the criticism. Overall, skilled techniques of communication are not being used.

According to my research, it is crucial for you as a woman to be able to discuss your issues openly with your husband. You never want to get to the place in your marriage where you are seriously dissatisfied or are cheating. Let's consider the most effective way to communicate your concerns to your husband so you can avoid ever getting to that place.

To begin, you'll want to have a carefully constructed plan ready before meeting with your husband so that you'll get your concerns across in such a way that you can enact change. I explore concrete steps to help you create a plan in the next several pages. For the good of the relationship, you must first be as clear as possible, with your husband and yourself, about your personal issues with the relationship. One woman in my study said she kept telling her husband to "appreciate me" more, and when he did that, it fell flat. It was only later, and unfortunately through her cheating, that she came to learn that a completely different, crucial piece of her marriage was missing. When things are going wrong in a relationship, all of us tend to just feel awful and everything bad gets completely mixed up inside. We often lose clarity about what the specific problems are, and no longer know where to even start to fix them.

I sent thank-you messages to many of the women who participated in my research. I was grateful they had taken the time to write their stories or complete the rather lengthy list of questions about whether they were faithful or unfaithful. I was surprised when many of them expressed thanks to me for just allowing them to take the survey. They explained that it had helped them assess clearly what was going on in their marriage. What I hadn't realized was that the research itself was a way for women to seriously evaluate their issues and help them decide what if any problems needed to be addressed.

You probably don't want to sit with your husband and have a wonderful, successful discussion about changes in your relationship, only to find out that you've made an error and that other issues are the real problem. But sometimes that's a necessary part of the process, as attempting changes that fail can help you find the real problem.

It's prudent—I dare say necessary—that before you approach your husband, you take the survey on pages 206 to 213 to help you identify what's bothering you. After that, we'll discuss how you can approach your husband in a way that is most likely to have him agree to make changes.

For some of these questions, you'll have several answers that you have to rate with percentages, so you'll have to identify which issues are really the most important. You may have lots of issues, but you surely can't bring up every one when you meet with your husband. You want to focus on those that are most difficult for you. Men need specifics, not generalizations. They need details, not the big picture. They like to solve a problem, as we discussed, so to make changes they need as much detailed information as possible so that together with you they can create a clear plan of change.

Self-Assessment Relationship Questionnaire for Women

Regardless of how your relationship is going, the first thing you as a woman need to do to make it better is to have a clear understanding of what your personal issues are within your marriage. Answering these questions will help you identify areas that you'll want to focus on in order to make your marriage better.

1. Sum up the pressing issues in your marriage (if any). (Choose one response.)

    _____ I currently have no serious problems with my husband.

    _____ Issues related to our unsatisfying sexual relationship outweigh my emotional dissatisfaction with our relationship.

    _____ Issues related to emotional dissatisfaction in our marriage outweigh an unsatisfying sexual relationship.

    _____ Both emotional dissatisfaction and an unsatisfying sexual relationship figure about the same.

    _____ I have other issues that are unrelated to either sexual or emotional aspects of my marital relationship. (Please explain: _____)

2. What are the specific emotional issues that you currently
    have with your husband? (Please choose all that apply, des-
    ignating a percentage value so that your answers add up to
    100 percent. Even if your response to question 1 was that
    you do not have "serious" issues with your husband, please
    respond with your minor issues here.)

    _____ My husband does not spend enough time with me.

    _____ When I share my thoughts and feelings, my hus-
    band does not understand me, does not address my
    issues, or is not willing to talk about them further.

    _____ I feel underappreciated by my husband, and he is
    not sufficiently thoughtful and caring toward me.

    _____ He rarely or never makes plans to be with me or
    focus on our marriage.

    _____ Other aspects of my husband's life (such as his
    career, community responsibilities, our children,
    and so on) are more important to him than our
    relationship.

    _____ We are no longer interested in the same things.

    _____ My husband often loses his temper and is frequently
    moody, angry, hostile, and so on.

    _____ Other: _____

    _____ I have no emotional issues with my husband.

3. What are the specific sexual issues that you currently have
    with your husband? (Please choose all that apply, designat-
    ing a percentage value so that your answers add up to 100
    percent. Even if your response to question 1 was that you
    have no "serious" issues with your husband, please respond
    with your minor issues here.)

    _____ Sex with my husband is unsatisfying.

_____ My husband significantly neglects his appearance.

_____ My husband demands too much sex or makes other sexual requests I am uncomfortable with.

_____ Sex with my husband is generally too infrequent.

_____ I have no sexual issues with my husband.

_____ Other:_____

4. In the past six months, I have had sex with my husband on average per month _____ times.

   Am I satisfied with this number? _____ Yes   _____ No

5. In the past six months, how often have you been angry at your partner?

   _____ A lot

   _____ Sometimes

   _____ Hardly

   _____ Not at all

6. Have you seriously considered divorce or separation in the past year?

   _____ Yes

   _____ No

7. Was anyone ever sexually inappropriate toward you at any point from birth until age twenty?

   _____ No

   _____ Yes

   Please explain. (Some people find it therapeutic to write about it and see it right there in front of them, but please skip this step if this makes you uncomfortable.) _____

   _____

   _____

   _____

If you have been molested, consider how it as affects your trust of your husband and how it may affect you sexually. You'll want to discuss how to make sex more comfortable for you.

8. The main reason(s) I have not had an infidelity is: (Check all that apply. Answer this question only if you have remained faithful.)

_____ I work hard on my marriage and feel close with my husband.

_____ My religious beliefs prevented me.

_____ I know how much it would hurt my husband.

_____ The opportunity hasn't presented itself.

_____ I'm afraid of getting caught.

_____ Other: _____

9. I have experienced the following stressors in the past six months of my married life: (Please check off as many as apply.)

_____ Financial strains

_____ Job-related pressures

_____ My own personal health problems

_____ Health problems of a close friend or family member

_____ Problems related to child-rearing

_____ Problems related to my parents or extended family

_____ Problems related to my in-laws or my husband's extended family

_____ None of the above

_____ Other: _____

10. My husband and I attempted therapy:

_____ Fewer than three sessions

_____ Three to ten sessions

_____ More than ten sessions

_____ We did not attempt marital therapy

_____ We have had no reason to attempt marital therapy

11. I felt these sessions were: (Answer this question only if you have attended therapy.)

_____ Helpful

_____ Generally unproductive. Please explain: _____

_____

_____

12. If no therapy ever took place, it was: (Answer this question only if you have not attended therapy.)

_____ Requested by my husband and I refused.

_____ Requested by me and my husband refused.

_____ Never seriously discussed.

_____ Our marriage was/is good enough that therapy was never needed.

13. If my husband would ever bring up the idea of my having an infidelity, I would tell him that:

_____ I would never do that.

_____ I don't plan to but no one can be sure in that area.

_____ Other: _____

14. How often have you and your husband talked alone on a daily basis, on average, in the past six months?

_____ Five minutes or less per day

_____ Five to fifteen minutes per day

_____ Fifteen to thirty minutes per day

_____ Thirty to sixty minutes

_____ Over sixty minutes

Are you satisfied with the amount of time you spend alone together?

_____ Yes

_____ No

15. How satisfied are you currently in your marriage or relationship?

_____ Extremely satisfied

_____ Satisfied

_____ Dissatisfied

_____ Extremely dissatisfied

16. If I could, I would:

(Check all that apply)

_____ Spend less time focused on my job and more time focused on my marriage.

_____ Spend less time focused on household work/children and more time focused on my marriage.

_____ Go out with my husband more frequently.

_____ Try to communicate more openly with my husband.

_____ Spend less time online or with other personal activities and more time with my husband.

_____ Take better care of myself.

_____ Get myself and my husband some form of counseling.

_____ None of the above

_____ Other: _____

17. When I got married:

_____ I never thought I would have an infidelity.

_____ I thought it was a possibility that I would have an infidelity.

_____ I told my husband that it was a possibility that I would have an infidelity.

_____ I thought it was a possibility but told my husband I would never have an infidelity.

_____ I thought it was a possibility but avoided the topic of infidelity anytime my husband brought it up.

18.   I am aware of individuals who have had an infidelity including: (Please check off as many as apply.)

_____ Immediate family members

_____ Close friends

_____ Acquaintances

_____ Coworkers

Consider if and how your response to question 18 may be affecting you and your feelings for your relationship.

19.   I perceived my parents' marriage as generally:

_____ Positive

_____ Negative

_____ Negative and filled with conflict

Consider whether you have repeated any similar negative issues in your own relationship or whether you have taken the lessons of your parents' marriage and expected the same from your own relationship.

20.   I would recommend that my husband: (Please place a number percentage value so that your answers add up to 100 percent. Even if you responded earlier that you have no serious issues with your husband, please respond with your minor issues here.)

_____ Make more time to spend together as a couple.

_____ Be more appreciative of me.

_____ Have more sex with me.

_____ Be more open to trying additional sexual play.

_____ Be willing to talk to me more about my thoughts and feelings.

_____ Be more even-tempered.

_____ Get himself/us into some form of counseling.

_____ None of the above

_____ Other: _____

Review your assessment. It will help you identify the specific issues you need to present to your spouse, and how you can discuss the changes you need to make. It will also help you decide what you may need to do differently. Write notes next to the questions that you'd like to address during your conversation, brainstorming some ideas about how you'd like to see your relationship change in that specific area.

The Conversation He'll Listen To

Proceed with this conversation in the form of a structured meeting. There should be a calm atmosphere in which you and your husband are not rushed, hungry, or tired.

1. Start by explaining that whatever you're about to discuss it's because you love him and want both of you to be happy and get more out of your relationship. If you didn't care, you'd be happy to be left alone. You're talking to him because you don't want this relationship to settle in a place where both of you are distant. Remind him that both of you came together out of love and no matter how far away you are

from that time, you want to give yourselves a real chance at getting back to a loving place for both of you.

It's important that he see this meeting as something for him as well as you. Some men hear a woman wanting to talk and think, "Yeah, what else do I have to do for you now?" or "What did I do now?" They need to be reminded that this talk is for them just as much as for you, because they will get all of the benefits of emotional and physical intimacy and a better relationship. Be clear about how you want things to be great. You want more love, more sex, more fun. Emphasize that paying attention will result in things that will be great for both of you. Keep in mind that you called this meeting, so he might not have put nearly as much effort into assessing the relationship as you have. He likely has his own work to do to consider what his issues are and how he might want to discuss them.

2. Have a pad and paper at the meeting. Too many couples talk out issues, even cry together as they reaffirm their love, have a meaningful night, have terrific sex, and then it's really nice for about for about three days until they're even more hopelessly disappointed because nothing substantive has changed. There was no resolution. Men are trained to be good at meetings where they solve issues. Writing down the issues you discuss and creating a list of possible solutions makes your meeting about something real. It may sound strange because so few people do this when they talk about their personal relationships. But it's probably what a therapist would do if you were to attend therapy. In counseling it's normal to have pads and pens around to write lists, ideas, and solutions, because that's how many of us focus on the topics being discussed.

Paper and pen mean that you and your partner are taking this seriously, looking hard at issues, and committing to change. You can refer back to your notes from the meeting, as you would after any good business meeting, the next time you meet with each other about these issues. Everyone is more likely to follow through with their commitments when things are written down and can't be waved away with "I don't remember that," or "That's not how we meant it." When we write, we show we're not playing around and we're going to treat this as a meeting to solve issues.

3. Before you tell him your issues, first explain that you don't have the answers or want to dictate any conclusions. You are looking to just throw it out to him so that both of you can figure out a solution. Men love to solve problems, so let him put these on his plate and together you can discuss possible solutions. Be prepared to hear his issues as well and be open to considering changes he might ask you to make. He might say he doesn't get you gifts because you return them, or he doesn't initiate sex because you were upset the last time the two of you had sex and he didn't please you, or he doesn't pay you compliments because when he does you tell him to stop talking about your body instead of your other qualities. Don't become defensive, but jot his thoughts down on paper and consider them carefully. You can tell him your side of these events, but try to feel comfortable taking responsibility for your actions as well. That can make it easier for him to take responsibility for his actions. If you get defensive and angry, how do you expect him to react? Model the behavior you'd like to see from him. Put him in a problem-solving mood. Tell him he's great at solving issues and that even though you are raising some criticisms of him, you are willing to hear his criticisms of you and you want to talk about solutions as a loving couple.

4. Develop a plan for change. It doesn't have to be a complete plan, but some commitment to some change, no matter how small, is necessary. You want to exit this meeting with a feeling that not only did you clearly communicate openly but you at least began the process of change. This commitment puts both of you in the right frame of mind: our relationship is valuable and needs to be nurtured. This relationship deserves our ongoing attention and discussion.

5. Don't stop at your calm, open communication. Making your relationship better deserves another meeting. It could be a month away or a week away. Obviously, if your relationship is in jeopardy in any way, a meeting sooner rather than later is important to maintain this rhythm of working on your issues together. Now both of you know that you've made commitments, some issues have been expressed in writing, and you'll be meeting soon to assess what each of you has done and where to go from there. Setting a date for the next meeting will make you both accountable, because you'll know that you're expected to be prepared to discuss what you have done to follow through with your commitments.

6. Be crystal clear if he's unwilling to listen. Men don't like threats, but sometimes they need to see the writing on the wall. Too many women have told me things like, "You know, I should have threatened to leave him," or "I should've left him a long time ago because when I did leave, he suddenly got serious and was willing to make enormous changes." If your husband is unwilling to even have a meeting with you, or if you find that he's not taking the meeting seriously and is flatly unwilling to join you, let him know that his lack of cooperation is dangerous to your relationship. You could say

something like, "I'm not threatening, but let's face facts: the odds of this relationship not working out are going to rise if we can't have an honest discussion about our issues with the intention of finding solutions and making things better for both of us." This puts him on notice.

It doesn't mean you can cheat, but it does mean that you know in your heart that there was at least one clear moment when you approached him with calmness and love and without anger and fighting. Hopefully, approaching him in this manner will cause him to return to you with greater resolve to hear what you have to say. If not, his refusal to listen is going to severely hamper your ability to have a better relationship. It doesn't mean that you can't make things better by trying other techniques, such as the ones in this book and my other ones. Often one person taking the lead in a relationship can bring about wonderful changes. But if he won't listen to any of your issues even when you approach him with goodwill, it indicates that he's a type of man who may find change hard and something he generally doesn't want to consider under any circumstances. If you have a husband who refuses to meet you in this way, face it. This doesn't mean you have to leave him. You can choose to stay for kids or any other reason that may work for you. But you can't make believe he is trying and it's going to get better, when it's not. You can't keep putting yourself in a hopeless situation, making yourself vulnerable to a man who has clearly indicated to you that he's not going to even consider working or putting effort into your relationship.

You may see other indications of his willingness to work at the relationship. Perhaps he won't meet with you, but the next day he is more loving or caring because he saw you had some issues. If he needs a different forum to deal with these issues, he's entitled to offer that suggestion. But if he just flatly refuses to listen to you, know it and deal with it in an honest way. Seeing a counselor by yourself, as it's likely he'll refuse to join you, is a good next step.

These steps offer ways to treat your communication with honesty and dignity. It's not something that you throw around in the midst of an argument. Take the time to really analyze your relationship first, discover your issues, and bring these issues to your husband. This approach will set the right tone for positive change and nurturing of your relationship as well as creating a commitment for both of you to properly care for your love.

12

How Men Can Choose to Have a Great Relationship

Men are good at making decisions. They tend to be confident even though everyone knows that no decision is anything but an educated guess. Men have been trained to be potential leaders. As we discussed at the start of this book, it's a common belief that men do not read relationship books and relegate such literature to women. Too many men see the women in their lives as the relationship leader, and are not proactive in making the relationship better. If it fails, they tend to blame the woman, even though they know that if they didn't do anything to make something work, they shouldn't complain when it breaks.

Bottom line: Your relationship is about both of you. Unlike other individual responsibilities, it isn't one that can be delegated to just one of you. If you want the love you hoped for, it'll require your personal and focused attention, just like anything else in your life in which you seek success. Your relationship isn't much different from business or sports. It demands attention and teamwork. That's obvious, but since men are not trained in relationships the same way they are in business and sports, they just find a way to focus their thoughts elsewhere.

A wonderful thing happens when you decide to make your relationship a priority: you create a loving environment. You can't make your relationship perfect or exactly what you want, but when you put consistent energy into it, it changes the "feel" of the connection between you and your wife. Because you both feed off each other's energy, there will be no limit to what the two of you can build and enjoy. So take the time to seriously consider what you want from your relationship, and make the decision to become a crucial part of it, if you haven't already. Just like business and sports, if it's not working for you, get involved. It's your only chance of making it better. Complete the self-assessment relationship questionnaire in the next section to help you get started and clarify what you can do to make your relationship better right now.

Self-Assessment Relationship Questionnaire for Men

- What are the primary ingredients for me to be successful in my career?
- Do I generally apply these ingredients to my marriage on a regular basis?

- On an average daily basis, how much time do I spend working and thinking about work-related issues?

- On an average daily basis, how much uninterrupted time do I spend on work?

- On an average daily basis, how much uninterrupted time do I spend with my wife alone?

- On an average daily basis, how much time do I spend thinking about my wife or my marriage?

- How many times a week do I consider making a change in my behavior or thinking in order to better profit financially?

- How many times a week do I consider making a change in my behavior or thinking in order to better profit in my relationship?

- If I received two seminar invitations given on the same day, one for making more money and the other for having a better marriage, which one would I prefer to attend?

- What is my goal for my marriage at this time?

- What have I done in the last month to accomplish this goal?

- Do I care enough about my wife (and children) to read this book with the intention of understanding my wife better and taking responsibility to do everything I can to make this relationship better?

- If this relationship were my business, what advice would I give myself as a consultant?

- What would my wife say she wants from me and what has stopped me from following through on her requests?

Now review your answers. Are you truly giving your relationship the energy it needs? Surely you realize that you will personally benefit from having a wonderful marriage. The rewards are much more varied than you think. Not only will you be happier, but a 2010 study showed that a successful marriage can affect your health as well. The study, which followed over ten thousand men from 1963 to 2008, revealed that single men or unhappily married men were 64 percent more likely to have a fatal stroke than happily married men. Commit to making some changes based on the results of your self-assessment for just one week, then at the end of that week, reevaluate to see how much your marriage has improved.

Changing your attitude toward your relationship may involve doing things you don't feel like doing, but give yourself a chance. We all do things we don't feel like doing when we feel there's a good reason for it. Look at your job as a prime example. Being successful there takes work and focus. Why should your love life fall short because it's hard to be attentive to it? If you commit yourself to making changes, you'll be reducing the odds of ever experiencing the horrible feeling that comes with divorce or cheating, by you or her. And that's not my opinion. It's based on my research. Too many men only come to grips with what they have to do when some tragedy strikes in the marriage. Here is your chance, if tragedy hasn't already happened, to change your marriage for the better.

And as I said in chapter 10, the changes suggested in this book that you make for the sake of your relationship are good for you as an individual. They enable you to look inside yourself and come to a deeper understanding of the causes of your problems. You can then free yourself from the old ways of thinking that stand in the way of you truly connecting with the woman you love. If your wife has given you this book, start showing her that you care enough about your relationship with her to read it, for her sake, for yours, and if you have any children, for their sake too.

PHIL'S STORY
Almost a Lifetime without
the Love I Could Have Had

I don't think I was uncaring or mean or anything, but I was hardly thinking of my wife. We'd been married twenty-seven years and had two kids, one in college and another who was almost there. It was my second marriage so I was almost ready to retire. It was a perfect plan. Kids moving out, a proper retirement, enough to get a place in Florida and play golf into the sunset. It was after midnight when *Oprah* was rebroadcast and I saw your show on men cheating. I felt sick to my stomach. It was when that guy took a lie detector test and passed that it struck me. I'm not sure why, but the next morning I approached my wife in the kitchen and asked her straight out if she ever cheated. She said she had, just like that. It was surreal because neither of us seemed mad. Hell, I had no idea what to do. I knew everything had gone, every dream, every part of the plan. I knew things weren't good and much worse, obviously, but I just guess I didn't think about it. I don't have a good answer. When I saw the show it jogged that strange gut feeling you let yourself have sometimes.

We sat and talked, and it makes me sick to say it, but it was probably the most honest, caring conversation we'd had in years. We both sat there and cried, knowing we were stuck with no idea of what to really do. She had become a stranger to me. All that time I had thought she was low-maintenance and didn't need a lot of my time to hear her go on about her day. But it had nothing to do with anything other than that she was getting all that somewhere else. Luckily, they had ended it a few years back. I'm sure if it was still active, we would've just divorced. But since neither of us had anything better on the horizon, we thought maybe we could make it work.

We have. It's not been easy. Some days I'm very angry at her and other days I'm really mad at myself. But I'm finally getting over all of the anger and beginning to enjoy my marriage for the first time. My kids are now in their own relationships and comment usually in a joking way how much more time I spend with her now. We'll work it out, but I don't know if I'll ever get over kicking myself for almost a lifetime wasted without the love I could've had, right in my own home.

Men and Anger

When men get angry, it can be alarming to women. I've sat in my office when a man has raised his voice and had his wife look at me and say, "See his anger, see how he's yelling?" and I never noticed it. Being a man, when he raised his voice, I didn't perceive it as yelling, but his wife did hear it that way. Whether we'd like to face it or not, men are the "stronger" and more aggressive gender. When a man yells, it is taken more seriously than when a woman yells at the same pitch. Again, this doesn't mean it's okay for women to be inappropriately angry or that there aren't angry women who are dangerous. But by and large, men can get angry in a way that is scary to women. This anger is a good thing when he is protecting loved ones or facing an enemy in war. Unfortunately, it's rather disastrous for relationships. Some women who normally wouldn't adopt a shouting style of fighting start shouting back when they feel they are being yelled at. Think to yourself, how is this going to end up? With a family culture of scary shouting all around.

When you express anger through shouting, an unfortunate thing occurs. The focus of the moment surrounds your angry reaction, rather than the issue you are angry about. Here's a hypothetical case. A guy really loses it and starts shouting at his wife, "I can't believe you have me waiting out here in the snow while you're inside on the phone with your mother . . . I can't stand your mother . . ." and so on. He has only made things worse. He may really have a point. He was left waiting outside in the cold because his wife was talking to her mother whom she talks to four times a day. But there's no way for that conversation to lead to any difference in how they treat each other. It's going to be about his anger control, and the only way for the marriage to last is for him to apologize and commit to change while the real issue of how they treat each other is lost.

This way of expressing your anger could be damaging to your relationship, because you may have important points to make but because you choose to yell, the points will get lost and the focus will be on your anger. Your point may be valid but the intensity of your reaction is invalid. This happens frequently with men, making it impossible to find solutions for the problems they want to resolve, because the topic quickly moves on to their anger.

Check your anger. If your wife is feeling uncomfortable, stop it. It doesn't matter if you feel she's taking it the wrong way or over-reacting. If she's uncomfortable, you'll never get across any point other than that you're trying to control the situation through anger. Calm yourself by taking a break and perhaps writing down your thoughts to give to her, or to discuss with her later if that is more workable. Consider your relationship as you would your job. Everyone screaming at each other isn't going to provide the mood to truly work out your issues and listen to each other. Be aware of your anger and find alternate ways to express it other than by yelling and engaging in other angry nonverbal behaviors.

The *Oprah* show asked me to travel to Minnesota to counsel Timothy and Amy through their economic crisis. After Timothy lost his six-figure job and couldn't find another, he became angry and admitted to walking around the house grumpy and expressing his anger about money at his wife. He soon became depressed, and after one year of his being somewhat unable to function due to his depression and his unwillingness to get any kind of help, his wife left him.

I asked Timothy to go back to the time before his depression when he was angry and yelling at Amy.

"If you could've expressed yourself well instead of just throwing your anger around at Amy, what would you have said to her?"

"I would've told her, 'I'm scared.'"

So many men use anger as a way to express what is uncomfortable for them to say calmly. But keeping feelings in and pretending to be strong when you feel weak is a recipe for confusion and anger. As a man, you can express feelings. You can say I'm scared, I'm nervous, I'm frustrated, I'm depressed, I'm sad, and still be seen as a man by your wife. A woman appreciates a man who can tell her how he feels instead of dressing it all up in anger and expressing it in a way that she has no ability to properly decipher or help with. As evidenced with Tim and Amy, a job loss or other crisis is best dealt with directly. As hard as it is for you, letting her know how you really feel can save your relationship.

Women Want to Be Desired

The research shows that women want to know that you want to spend time with them, appreciate them, understand their thoughts and feelings, and desire them sexually and engage in wonderful sex frequently. Overall they want to feel that they are a priority to you, and that even when you are away you are still connected to them, considering them, and looking forward to being with them. Typically when you do this, you are met with love, warmth, and support from the woman you are in love with. Women tend to respond to your genuine feelings with great understanding, and it allows the two of you to face challenges together.

When women don't get this, and feel you don't get them, there's a disconnect. And depending on the woman, the response to this disconnect has shown itself to be anything from sadness and depression, to seeking emotional connections elsewhere, to affairs and other forms of cheating, and finally, to rage. The rage may take the form of substance abuse, or something else. I've known the most giving and rational of women who have become full of rage in response to their husband's neglect. They do uncharacteristic things, from maxing out the credit cards to throwing objects against the wall. Again, I'm not excusing such behavior; I'm just saying what can happen. I think men just don't understand how hurt women can get and how personally they can take what they perceive as their husband's rejection. Those feelings of hurt can take them to places of great personal pain. Avoiding this pain can be as simple as sending the message to your wife that you desire her in every way.

Is She Really Your Financial Partner?

Men generally are regarded by the culture as breadwinners. Wives certainly work and earn money as well, but when society views the sum total of the economic side of any family, it looks to the man. As a result, many men unfortunately define themselves by the work they do or the money they make. If they are the primary wage earners, many men feel that the money belongs to them. They might be aware that they have to share the money with their wives and use some of it for the family, but they might still have a sense of entitlement that they feel their wives should not have. They might spend a certain amount of money, whether for a personal item or an investment, without conferring with their wives, even though they'd expect their wives to confer with them when making that sort of purchase.

Identify your true feelings on this matter. Many women feel that the money made is as much theirs as it is their husbands'. They believe that there was a deal struck along the way in the relationship that established the woman as the primary caregiver of the home and children while the man was to be the primary financial earner. Women see this as an agreed split, which naturally entitles a man to the same "ownership" over children as there would be in every other part of the relationship. One partner might have knowledge or experience in certain areas that the other respects and therefore agrees to follow that partner's position. A father might disagree with the mother's decision regarding a child-care issue but go along with it because he admits that she has more knowledge, experience, or time spent in that area. A wife might disagree with her husband's financial decision but choose to allow him to make it because she admits that he has more knowledge, experience, or time spent in that area.

The point is to allow both partners to feel that there is a partnership, and that demands a common respect and an agreement to properly discuss all major issues. When you make a major decision without discussing it seriously with your partner, you send a clear message that you are in charge and have greater dominance in that area. Is this the unspoken agreement you've created with your partner? Your relationship will thrive in a scenario that makes both of you feel equal on matters of importance to your relationship. You don't have to agree on every issue, just share all decisions the way you'd feel obligated to in a business partnership.

This question of equality speaks to a deeper issue for women. It's important to note that around the world there are legal restrictions on women even today that prohibit them from voting, driving, or leaving their homes without a male escort. These women don't live only in third-world villages; they live in sleek, modern air-conditioned buildings in countries that deny them basic rights. There are women bought and sold even today, and women everywhere in the past were regarded as chattel.

Women have developed almost a collective unconscious that (rightly) resists being made to feel "less than." They've been treated in a way that reduces them to beings made for service to men. Obviously, our own Western culture has come a long way to change this, but women are still correct in being sensitive to when they are made to feel less smart, less capable, and less deserving of respect. You may not know what it means to be constantly challenged, downtrodden, molested, or judged just because of your gender. It causes women to fight for the feeling of being a partner and to quickly become dismayed when their husbands give them the impression that they are anything less. You are with your wife because you love her and want to have her as your life partner. Treat her with that respect and honest regard, and you will have developed a true partnership that will allow both of you to learn from each other and ultimately make better decisions that will make you closer just for having the ability to share the decisions in the first place.

Consider the following questions:

1. Are you her chief cheerleader? Do you put your own insecurities aside and celebrate her successes? Are you there with the champagne and the toast? Or do you make it all about you and where you are in your career and undermine her with little "jokes" to put down her success?

2. Do you seek out time together? Do you do the activities she likes even if they aren't your first choice? Would you go out of your way more for your buddy than for her?

3. Are you cheap? Do you question every purchase she makes? Do you skimp on her comfort so that you can buy the best golf putter? An old Talmudic saying goes, "You can tell a man's character by how he handles three things: his wife, his anger, and his money." You can be frugal and still be generous to her.

4. When she's sick, are you there? Do you take care of things and let her get better? Do you cook or bring her food? Help her and make her laugh? Or do you gripe or become sullen, insisting she get up and around before she's ready?

5. Are you—how do I put this—a mean person? Are you the type to be rude to the waitress, be condescending to the janitor, confuse the puppy—you know, not a rageaholic, but mean in an insidious, soul-sapping way? Think about it. If you are, are you willing to go to therapy or talk to a clergyperson and discover what makes you that way and work to be kinder?

6. Are you interested in helping her with her problems? Whether it's finding the right outfit for a friend's wedding or helping her talk out an issue with her parent, do you take seriously what concerns her? Do you attack problems together or do you just attack her?

7. Does she come first and does she know that? Do you treat her well? Listen to what she wants and try to do it? Do you care about her opinions? If not, is it her or are you just generally uninterested in what anyone but you yourself thinks or wants?

8. Is living with you a giant challenge? Are you constantly bringing up big dramas and discussions at midnight when she's told you she isn't a night person? Do you blow huge sums of money on stupid things but deny her basics? Do

you consistently show up late, leave her at social events to mingle incessantly, and ignore her requests? Do you just do exactly what you want to without really listening to her and make jokes about how domineering and controlling she is and ignore your own passive-aggressive tendencies? Do you do the little errands she asks of you, saying sure you don't mind but later throw it in her face that she nags you and bothers you? Do you bring up her past mistakes to distract from the issue at hand? Are you inherently, pathologically dishonest with her? Are you a slob about hygiene?

9. Do you understand *why* some women carry an almost genetic disdain and maybe a little anger at how they're seen or treated? Do you know the history of women and that even today in otherwise civilized countries women are denied the right to drive a car, to vote, to be educated? Do you respect women's long road to equality? Do you demean them by making jokes and leering at attractive women?

As with every relationship, yours is going to be as wonderful as the energy you put into making it great. Be willing to take an honest look at yourself and become a better man to your wife. Just the effort alone will encourage her to bring her best self to the relationship as well.

EPILOGUE

Make Your Partner Feel Like Your Top Priority

We all want to be desired. Every one of us wants to be special to our partner and feel that we are exciting and their favorite person. What you do to make your partner feel that way can be the most important question you ask yourself. If both partners are asking that regularly, there's sure to be great growth and love.

When we make our partner feel special and desired, the most wonderful thing happens: we bring out the very best in him or her. Let's face it. All of us have a beautiful side and a less than beautiful side. Different people can bring out different aspects of ourselves because to some extent we're responding to how each person makes us feel. Whenever you improve yourself, it goes without saying that you'll likely improve your partner with your enlightened energy. Your partner feeds off your love and warmth. If the two of you are focused on being the best you can be, it's a recipe for great love and romance.

Bringing out the best in each other is also accomplished when a couple tastes new fruits together. When you both learn new things, travel to new places, create new experiences together, you give life to your relationship and protect it from growing stale. Many couples find time for everything new in other areas of their lives like work and child-related issues, with little concern for actually reserving something new for their relationship. But talk to happy couples, and you'll learn that they enjoy doing things together. They might have recently taken dance lessons, traveled, learned new technology, visited museums, read books, done low-key things like take in a foreign film. These activities create interest and sometimes excitement in the marriage. They allow a couple to laugh about and learn about each other along the way. You'd be surprised at how willing your partner may be when you suggest doing something new.

Whenever there is change, there is tremendous love. There is nothing harder than real change, and a willingness to do so for one's partner (while helping oneself as well) indicates great love. Unfortunately, change takes time and, as we've clearly outlined throughout this book, there are many steps along the way. One's willingness to change doesn't mean that change will happen quickly. So when your partner makes attempts but you still feel they're falling short of the goal, focus more on the love that is being expressed by the effort instead. The goal is important, but it can only be reached through a concerted effort. That is the sure sign of love.

Always remember that most couples go through ups and

downs in both life and their marriage. I'll often ask a couple who first comes to see me and is trying to decide if they should stay together whether they'd be able to have a nice time if I sent them on an all-expenses-paid vacation together. Most will answer yes immediately, but quickly follow it up with something like, "but that's not real life." This is another way of saying, "We can really love each other but we don't know how to bring that into our daily living." It shows, however, that even though these people are at the point where they are seriously considering divorce, they still have a friendship, a potential warmth, even a love. Some couples would no longer be able to vacation together due to so much hurt or distance over time. But for those who could, it's a simple lesson that many couples do belong together but haven't learned or focused on what partners want and need to make daily life a loving experience. If you are far from able to spend even stress-free time together, you're overdue for some form of therapy.

Lovers come together out of love and a willingness to try to enjoy life together. Too often, we fall far from that plan and lose the willpower to make it work, while instead we overwhelm ourselves with efforts to make so many other things work. Women want to be looked at the same way their men looked at them when they first fell in love. They want their husbands to have that excitement, that charge that was there in the beginning. All of us are realistic enough to know that it can't be like that every second of every day, but having the focus to maintain a lot of that is a must.

My dream has always been to help others. Hearing from over five hundred female voices for this book has given all of us the knowledge to create a happy relationship environment. The challenge of life is to grow and be better people. Take this challenge and work hard to love and bring love to your partner every day. It's not unusual for you to wake up and wonder what you can do today to forward your specific goals for your children or work.

Why not wake up each day and wonder, "What can I do today to put a smile on my partner's face?" Ultimately, your best effort comes from a willingness to confront yourself and make efforts to be a loving partner.

My research has offered you significant clarity regarding what a woman wants. The voices of over five hundred woman have spoken loudly for everyone to put energy into some clear, specific places. We now know statistically that the average happy woman:

- Spends significantly more time talking to her partner.

- Has twice as much sex as the unhappy woman.

- Is five times less angry.

- Is much more appreciated by her partner.

- Feels her thoughts are heard and understood.

- Is almost twice as likely as the unhappy woman to seek out therapy when there are issues, whether she has cheated or not.

This book has focused you on these areas and how to best and quickly make changes in these areas so that you benefit the most from your love relationship. I've also given you a path to really open up to yourself and your partner and see the deeper issues that might be holding you back from experiencing a great relationship. Using this technique will give you a renewed sense of control over your participation in your love life so that you can experience the love you want and deserve.

For a previous book, I interviewed many couples who were married more than forty years. All of them had great advice, but the one common denominator was that they all worked regularly on their marriage. Not one of them said it was easy or that they ever stopped focusing on it. Even after forty years, they still put effort into their love and reap the benefits of their efforts. As in my research, the number one answer (75 percent) of happily married women, when asked why they think they haven't cheated, was because they work hard on their marriage and feel close to their husbands. Clearly, chances of a happy relationship seriously increase when both spouses are tending to it.

Many happy women in my study shared their sense of firm commitment to their marriage. Not one that kept them feeling stuck but rather a commitment that helped them place their focus and energy on making love work for them. Whenever I start working with a couple, the first thing I do is get them to agree to a time period when they'll put aside their decisions about their couplehood and instead put all of their energy into their relationship. We explore what each one needs and the changes they have to make, but this can get quickly lost if every day turns into a "Based on today, how do I feel about this relationship?" That is an overwhelming pressure for anyone to have. After reading this book, whether as a couple or individually, make a time commitment to put the practical suggestions into effect without judging anything for three months or so. Give your loving relationship time to react to the changes, and keep your collective energy focused on making it better and not letting it be drained by a daily judgment of the big picture. The commitment itself is so empowering that it in itself fuels your strength to get ready to try new things and use the tools you've gained through this research and book.

Recently, I was asked by a magazine to sum up my relationship advice in one line. I suggested, "The one who gets you, gets you." The one who really gets you, who understands you deep down and wants to know everything about you, is the one who'll win your heart and soul. Make that one your partner, and you'll live a life full of love. Celebrate love, work to genuinely understand each other, and you will be forever connected to love.

APPENDIX A

Therapy Can Make a Difference

The judgment on therapy is still out. I know you wouldn't expect to hear that from someone who has been providing therapy for twenty-three years. But there is no cohesive, scientific proof that therapy works better than a host of other activities (like exercise) that people try in order to deal with complicated life issues. In fact, I've changed my opinion of going to therapy. Years ago I used to say that it might not help, but it doesn't hurt either. However, in my years as a therapist I have heard many stories from people who've had negative experiences with therapy. I now confidently believe that it *can* hurt, and I advise people to avoid it unless they have great recommendations for a therapist and feel from the start that it's helpful.

But let's not trash therapy altogether. My research revealed that therapy can make a difference. Forty-four percent of faithful women who reported having any problems sought out therapy. Compare that to 77 percent of cheaters who never attended therapy prior to their infidelity. Fifty-two percent never even seriously discussed therapy as an option. And only 22 percent of cheating women found therapy helpful before they cheated, compared to more than half of faithful women. Many faithful women found therapy helpful, perhaps because they reported attending more sessions than cheaters. Forty-six percent of cheaters, when asked what they would do differently if they could go back in time, answered, "Get myself and my husband some form of counseling." Unfortunately, 23 percent of the cheaters who didn't go to therapy had requested counseling and their partners refused.

When therapy is suggested, think about it carefully. Even if your partner isn't willing to attend, consider going yourself. It can help you gain a clear perspective on your relationship. You can learn a great deal about how you work as an individual and as a partner. Couples are about energy, and you can learn what energy you bring to the relationship that might have its ill effects. Sometimes the other partner will join in the therapy once he or she sees that you are serious about continuing with it. Make sure to set goals in your therapy from the start, and reassess every few sessions to see if it is helping you as much as you'd hoped.

APPENDIX B

Keeping Your Relationship
Safe at Work

We have learned from both of my studies that the number one place cheating men and women meet the other person is at work. Fifty-three percent of female cheaters met the man at work, while for men it was 40 percent. A much lower number for women, 13 percent, met the man while engaging in some activity of personal interest; and the percentages go down from there. Clearly, in addition to developing a strong, loving relationship with your partner, maintaining boundaries at work is crucial to ensuring your fidelity.

It makes perfect sense that the workplace affords a good setting for potential extramarital relationships. Work is where we put on a good front, dress our best, smile. We reserve many of our stressful and complicated feelings for the home environment. When we're sick and look like hell, we stay home. Work can be a place of pleasant chatter, since the stresses of life (money, kids, spouse) aren't staring us in the face. We can discuss those topics in a more relaxed, distant way. We have the mental space to talk about things in a way at work that we tend not to have at home. We are likely to spend much more time with coworkers than with our loved ones. We might take more meals together, have more lively conversations, and offer more warm gestures to those at work than to those at home. Sometimes, our work relationships are how our love relationships should be and once were.

I'm not suggesting you assume a curled-up, catatonic position in the corner of the room every time a member of the opposite sex enters your work environment. But we are often required not only to spend time with members of the opposite sex, but to be sensitive to them and to get to know them. A woman whose husband cheated on her once called me on a radio show to criticize office "team building" activities. Her husband's company had taken the employees on a full-day trip to a nearby city for sports and a lecture. Spouses were not invited. It was on that trip that her husband met the woman he went on to have an affair with, the woman he would later divorce his wife for. Perhaps he would have strayed anyway, but this activity certainly opened the door.

If we've learned anything of late, it's that work is not going to always be there for us. The days of companies "taking care" of employees are pretty much over. The office is definitely not your home away from home. Home is where the people who truly love you are. If you're lucky, you've forged good friendships at work, and although there are exceptions to every rule, it's your loved ones who will be there for you after the office is closed or you've been let go.

When sexual relationships take place, often it's after an intimacy and understanding have been reached. The average woman was dissatisfied in her relationship for five years before having an affair. That was the time to realize needs were going unmet at home. That's when you have the meeting about the relationship and take whatever steps (such as marital therapy) you need to take. When there is something going wrong at home, many people look to others to satisfy needs and desires. Both men and women in my studies have been clear that the large majority of the time, infidelity begins with an emotional connection. When a strong emotional bond develops, it often finds itself segueing into sex.

Our relationships demand that we draw and maintain boundaries for ourselves, especially at work. There were many responses to my last book, and an overwhelming number of women felt I hadn't emphasized boundaries enough. They felt men (and women as well) should maintain boundaries at work and take responsibility for controlling themselves. I agree, and my book *Emotional Infidelity* outlines how careful we need to be in these situations. I think we need to be aware of our relationships with the opposite sex since in many cases they can lead to escapes from our significant other. At the least, they inhibit our growth and intimacy in the relationship at home; at worst, they supplant that relationship.

Everyone knows what is meant by boundaries. If it doesn't feel right and like something you would do in front of your significant other, stop it. Here are some ways to maintain boundaries:

Be honest with yourself. We lie to ourselves sometimes. We say we're just being friendly, supportive, a mentor in the workplace. Ask yourself, would you be comfortable behaving this way if your partner were standing next to you? Sexuality can be masked with little competitive streaks and sniping between people too. Be aware of the effect someone has on you.

Avoid real intimacy. While it's good to be warm, sensitive, and kind in the workplace, work really isn't the setting for the kind of intimacy we should enjoy in our real friendships and love life. There's a big difference between listening to someone and giving advice and sharing your own deeper personal issues and problems. Once you share a lot of yourself, that's when intimacy can develop.

Keep it all business. Avoid going out for the evening to celebrate without your partner. Try to engage in group activities or meetings, and avoid one-on-one extended alone time when possible. Definitely limit alcohol consumption and anything that lowers inhibitions in settings where you might find your principles compromised. Discuss and agree upon a plan with your partner about how you will manage being away at a conference, especially during the downtime between sessions.

If you find yourself seriously considering acting out on an attraction you may feel, that's the time to be especially cautious and work on getting what you want from your partner. The attraction is a wake-up call that your primary relationship needs immediate nurturing or change.

APPENDIX C

Women Who Stray

We've learned that 39 percent of women cheat, and that, sadly, only 30 percent of women are happy in their relationships overall. Often, knowing the facts about unfaithfulness can renew your awareness and help you to look within yourself and your relationship to see if your couplehood is on a dangerous track.

Cheating Signals

Women in the study described the cheating signals they think they gave to their husbands that they were about to cheat and were cheating. The amazing lesson was that there was only a slight difference between the two. The top answers were the same. (Keep in mind that for these answers, women were asked to check off as many as applied.)

	About to Cheat	Already Cheating
Diminished sexual activity	42%	49%
More time spent away from home	48%	47%

(continued)

(continued)	About to Cheat	Already Cheating
Less time spent alone together talking with my husband	51%	47%
Avoidance of contact (e.g., cell phone calls)	40%	44%
More criticism of him	31%	31%
Starting more fights with him	24%	27%

It's telling that women felt that there wasn't much change in their marriage even after they started cheating. It speaks to the probability that the marriage was at such a sad place—the couple already suffered sexually, spent time away from home independent of each other, and spent little time talking that upon cheating their marriage didn't really change much. There was a slight (7 percent) spike in the diminished sexual activity category, but other than that, the marriage continued on the same.

The good news is that you can tell when your relationship is in danger. Perhaps you don't want to think about it and are too busy filling your life with other activities. Too many people want to explain away their problems by saying things like, "This is what marriage is like," and "My friends complain about the same things." You are probably right, because we've learned that the majority of marriages are failing. But don't take the "norm" to mean that what's going on in your marriage isn't an indicator of probable disaster. When you see the emotional and physical distance in your relationship, take it as the signal that your couplehood is in danger, whether from cheating or divorce.

Isn't it equally fascinating that only 49 percent of women said that there was diminished sexual activity after they started their infidelity? Wouldn't you think that would be a significantly higher number? The women who had affairs did report having sex an average of four times per month before cheating. I'm sure that among the half of cheaters who did not check off diminished sexual activity, some had sex fewer than four times a month with their husbands. But there must be some who still continued to have sex with their husbands even after having sex outside the marriage. As women wrote to me, the sex they were having with their husbands had no intimacy. It was about satisfying sexual urges and needs, and had little relationship attached to it. In this way, sex stayed the same for some even after finding sex with a different man.

How Many Years of Marriage Before the Cheating Began?

How long were women unhappy in their marriages before they started cheating? The average was a little over five years, plenty of time for either spouse to become aware of issues and make changes. If you're reviewing your relationship and you see things have been unhappy for a while, there's likely more time to work things out. But this statistic explains that there's a point at which a woman feels the distance has settled in and there is little hope of resolution. After five years of an unhappy marriage, these women made the mistake of looking elsewhere.

From the responses to my detailed research questions, I can begin to give you a picture of the marriage and life circumstances of the average cheating woman. After dating her husband for a couple of years, she gets married around age twenty-three. (She rarely cheats during engagement, although 16 percent do.) After a few decent years of marriage, the unhappiness sets in, leading the woman to choose to be unfaithful in her early thirties. The average age at which a cheating woman has her first or only affair is thirty-one, and typically it's with a man who is thirty-five. She has been married for about eight years before her infidelity. She already has one or two children, and her oldest is around seven or eight. She married never intending to cheat; 84 percent of cheaters never thought they'd end up having an infidelity.

Sixty-two percent have an infidelity with one man, while 36 percent cheat with more than one man and 2 percent cheat with another woman. Fifty-nine percent of the infidelities last less than one year.

How Long from Meeting to Cheating

Forty-seven percent of female cheaters had sex with the man after knowing him for six months or less. There is not as much time as one may think. Luckily, the average cheating woman is dissatisfied in her relationship for five years before cheating, which gives every couple much time to act and make positive changes.

How Long I Knew the Man I Cheated with before Having Sex

Less than one month	13%
One to six months	34%
Six to twelve months	16%
One to two years	11%
Two to five years	7%
Over five years	17%

(2% reported sexual cheating but not actual intercourse)

Do Cheaters Stay Married?

Sixty-two percent of the cheating women are currently married (although not necessarily to the man they cheated on) compared to 87 percent of the faithful women who reported being married.

Either the cheating or the personalities involved in those marriages explains the 25 percent difference between the groups. Faithful women stay married much more than cheating women.

Thirty-four percent of cheating women do not experience any guilt during the affair. This connects with another part of the research that indicated that 35 percent of women knew or suspected that their husbands were cheating. A woman has less guilt when she believes her spouse is cheating or has cheated.

Nineteen percent experienced guilt only at the onset of the affair, 29 percent had the guilt continue throughout, and 13 percent said their guilt escalated as the affair continued (5 percent listed "other"). It's hard to determine the role of guilt in these women's lives. Do we say that the guilt is not enough to stop them from cheating, or perhaps it is enough to cause the majority of them to end the affair in less than a year?

Guilt is a questionable feeling because it speaks to personal judgment. Am I right or wrong, and how do I determine that? Marriage vows seem to be clear about not cheating, but what if the other spouse has already cheated, is verbally abusive, or largely neglects the marriage? Divorce, you say. Good idea, and more than half of faithful woman have seriously considered that. But throw into the mix the fears over what divorce may do to the children, and suddenly many spouses feel stuck and make an unhealthy choice.

I'm not looking to justify cheating, but women who cheat may seek to justify their actions. They may feel some guilt, but because the marriage has usually been bad for many years, they may not use that guilt to guide them. They may want to see where an affair takes them; and for most of them, it doesn't take them too far because it ends in less than a year.

Guilt is an indicator to each of us that something is up. Sometimes it is misplaced, a standard that we don't personally agree with but were made to feel some way by a parent, or mentor. But often we feel guilty because we have determined somewhere deep inside that what we are about to do or have done isn't right. That's supposed to help guide us and seriously reconsider what is going on in our lives. Use your guilt to help you. We all know that sometimes we can feel guilty when we shouldn't (vacationing with your spouse and leaving the kids home), but the guilt is there to help us take a serious look (perhaps Grandma is too old to care for the three little ones even for a few days).

Whenever you feel that pang of guilt, think of it as your personal red flag. Use it to help you make healthier decisions. Or at the very least, talk to someone you trust (but not the person with whom you're considering cheating). Talking to someone can help you take a new look at your whole situation. Maybe you haven't tried everything in your relationship. Maybe there's a different way to go. Maybe you can accomplish your goal without doing something that'll cause you guilt. Don't ignore guilt. You don't have to make decisions based on it, but you can use it to make much better decisions.

Do Cheating Friends Influence Her?

Unlike men, women do not seem to be as influenced by their close friends. In my study of men, 77 percent of cheaters reported having best friends who cheated. But a little less than half of faithful men reported the same. Cheating men were 30 percent more likely to have a cheating best friend, which made it prudent for a man (and his wife) to watch his friendships and how they might be influencing him in this area. But it wasn't the same for women—yet another example of how careful we must be with society's presumptions. Sixty-three percent of cheating women reported having close friends who cheated. That was 12 percent more than faithful women, of whom 51 percent said their close friends cheated. That's still a difference, but is it significant enough to put worrying who a woman's friends are toward the top of our list of ways to avoid infidelity? Probably not, although people have to ask themselves if they are picking up some bad habits. If their friends are lying and cheating, do they see this as the norm or not so bad? There was no difference in each group as far as having immediate family members who cheated. Forty-eight percent of faithful women have family members who've cheated, and 49 percent of cheating women do as well.

From all of this research, you can begin to take a serious look at what women are saying. As we've learned, there's usually plenty of time before cheating may begin, even years, and plenty of signals. If you have your eyes wide open, you can look carefully at your relationship to see if it is falling into some of these patterns. That is always the first step. If you don't look at what is really going on in your life, you can never move to actually do anything about it. Looking back on their marriages, too many failed couples discuss cheating or divorce as if some alien being popped into their lives and forced something upon them.

As long as you stick your head in the sand, you can never make healthy changes. As uncomfortable as it may be, it's always better to look at the hand you're dealing with so you can fix it rather than to keep the cards face down and be shocked when the game doesn't play out the way you want. Empower yourself to look at your personal and relationship issues and use the techniques I've discussed to approach your partner with change.

INDEX